"This book is a lifeline for every mom [ ] advice to 'savor the season' or defeated b[ ] moment' of raising her kids—whether [be]cause of hard diagnoses, neurodiversity, complicated births, illness, loss, or just the average Tuesday. With gentleness and vulnerability, Katie Faris not only offers suffering mothers validation and permission to grieve their hardships but she also equips them to see their circumstances through the lens of Scripture, renewing their hope and confidence in God's goodness to them even and especially within the suffering with which they have been entrusted."

Abbey Wedgeworth, mom of three; author, *Held: 31 Biblical Reflections on God's Comfort and Care in the Sorrow of Miscarriage*

"Katie Faris shows us that parenting is not a pain-free experience, nor should that be our goal; it is a deep dependency on Christ. His strength is made perfect in weakness, and he is forming us through our grief and painful parenting experiences. Be encouraged: the gospel does indeed offer hope, comfort, and purpose in our journey."

Julie E. Lowe, Counselor and Faculty Member, Christian Counseling & Educational Foundation

"When the gift of motherhood is overshadowed by the grief of motherhood, we need a solid place to set our hope. Katie Faris helps us honestly engage our sorrows and points us to the only one who is enough to sustain and comfort us through them. If the trials of motherhood are overwhelming you and the heartache feels too heavy to bear, this book will be a balm to your weary heart, reminding you that God is still—and always will be—good. Read and find refuge in him."

Amy DiMarcangelo, author, *A Hunger for More: Finding Satisfaction in Jesus When the Good Life Doesn't Fill You*

"*God Is Still Good* helps moms to remember what our sorrows can help us to forget: we're neither alone nor without hope in Christ. In this book, Katie Faris serves readers as a conduit of God's comfort—a sympathetic sister who, as a result of her own painful trials in motherhood, has learned to lean on sustaining grace in the midst of desperation, grief, and disappointment. If you're a weary mother in need of encouragement—wondering how you're going to make it through the troubles of today—then the practical wisdom in this book is especially for you."

Christine Chappell, author, *Help! My Teen Is Depressed* and *Help! I've Been Diagnosed with a Mental Disorder*; Host, *Hope + Help Podcast*; certified biblical counselor

God Is Still Good

Other Gospel Coalition Books

A Better Encouragement: Trading Self-Help for True Hope, by Lindsey Carlson

Confronting Christianity: 12 Hard Questions for the World's Largest Religion, by Rebecca McLaughlin

Confronting Jesus: 9 Encounters with the Hero of the Gospels, by Rebecca McLaughlin

Demystifying Decision-Making: A Practical Guide, by Aimee Joseph

Everyday Faithfulness: The Beauty of Ordinary Perseverance in a Demanding World, by Glenna Marshall

Faithful Endurance: The Joy of Shepherding People for a Lifetime, edited by Collin Hansen and Jeff Robinson Sr.

Finding the Right Hills to Die On: The Case for Theological Triage, by Gavin Ortlund

Glory in the Ordinary: Why Your Work in the Home Matters to God, by Courtney Reissig

Gospel-Centered Youth Ministry: A Practical Guide, edited by Cameron Cole and Jon Nielson

Growing Together: Taking Mentoring beyond Small Talk and Prayer Requests, by Melissa B. Kruger

Keeping Your Children's Ministry on Mission: Practical Strategies for Discipling the Next Generation, by Jared Kennedy

Letters Along the Way: From a Senior Saint to a Junior Saint, by D. A. Carson and John D. Woodbridge

Mission Affirmed: Recovering the Missionary Motivation of Paul, by Elliot Clark

Missional Motherhood, by Gloria Furman

The New City Catechism

The Plurality Principle: How to Build and Maintain a Thriving Church Leadership Team, by Dave Harvey

Praying Together: The Priority and Privilege of Prayer: In Our Homes, Communities, and Churches, by Megan Hill

Rediscover Church: Why the Body of Christ Is Essential, by Collin Hansen and Jonathan Leeman

Seasons of Waiting: Walking by Faith When Dreams Are Delayed, by Betsy Childs Howard

Word-Filled Women's Ministry: Loving and Serving the Church, edited by Gloria Furman and Kathleen B. Nielson

God Is Still Good

*Gospel Hope and Comfort for the
Unexpected Sorrows of Motherhood*

Katie Faris

Foreword by Megan Hill

∷ CROSSWAY®

WHEATON, ILLINOIS

God Is Still Good: Gospel Hope and Comfort for the Unexpected Sorrows of Motherhood

Copyright © 2023 by Katie Faris

Published by Crossway
   1300 Crescent Street
   Wheaton, Illinois 60187

All rights reserved. No part of this publication may be reproduced, stored in a retrieval system, or transmitted in any form by any means, electronic, mechanical, photocopy, recording, or otherwise, without the prior permission of the publisher, except as provided for by USA copyright law. Crossway® is a registered trademark in the United States of America.

Cover design: Shutterstock

Cover image: Molly von Borstel

First printing 2023

Printed in the United States of America

Scripture quotations are from the ESV® Bible (The Holy Bible, English Standard Version®), copyright © 2001 by Crossway, a publishing ministry of Good News Publishers. Used by permission. All rights reserved. The ESV text may not be quoted in any publication made available to the public by a Creative Commons license. The ESV may not be translated into any other language.

All emphases in Scripture quotations have been added by the author.

Trade paperback ISBN: 978-1-4335-8238-7
ePub ISBN: 978-1-4335-8241-7
PDF ISBN: 978-1-4335-8239-4
Mobipocket ISBN: 978-1-4335-8240-0

Library of Congress Cataloging-in-Publication Data

Names: Faris, Katie, 1978– author.
Title: God is still good : gospel hope and comfort for the unexpected sorrows of motherhood / Katie Faris ; foreword by Megan Hill.
Description: Wheaton, Illinois : Crossway, 2023. | Includes bibliographical references and index.
Identifiers: LCCN 2022017677 (print) | LCCN 2022017678 (ebook) | ISBN 9781433582387 (trade paperback) | ISBN 9781433582394 (pdf) | ISBN 9781433582400 (mobipocket) | ISBN 9781433582417 (epub)
Subjects: LCSH: Mothers—Religious life. | Motherhood—Religious aspects—Christianity. | Consolation. | Expectation (Psychology)—Religious aspects—Christianity. | God (Christianity)—Goodness. | Hope—Religious aspects—Christianity.
Classification: LCC BV4529.18 .F35 2023 (print) | LCC BV4529.18 (ebook) | DDC 248.8/431—dc23/eng/20220804
LC record available at https://lccn.loc.gov/2022017677
LC ebook record available at https://lccn.loc.gov/2022017678

Crossway is a publishing ministry of Good News Publishers.

BP		32	31	30	29	28	27	26	25	24	23
15	14	13	12	11	10	9	8	7	6	5	4	3	2	1

Contents

This book is for all those who walk on
harrowing paths related to motherhood—
but especially my parents.
"So we do not lose heart. . . .
For this light momentary affliction is preparing
for us an eternal weight of glory beyond all comparison."

2 Corinthians 4:16–17

Foreword

Megan Hill

EVERY THURSDAY MORNING, a group of moms meets at our church. We call it "playgroup," as if it were for the good of the children, but really it's for the moms. It's our chance to laugh, to drink coffee, to share stories. The night before, we text one another a reminder: "Playgroup tomorrow, 10 a.m. See you there!" But when Thursday morning comes, we are never all there on time. One by one, long past ten, we each straggle in, explanations on our lips.

"I was all set to walk out the door, but my youngest tripped on the stairs."

"I would have been here earlier, but I had to run my teenager's lunch to the school."

"This was the week I was going to be on time, but the two-year-old decided not to sleep last night."

We offer these excuses as if the situations were unexpected, but this week's disruption is basically the same as last week's. If it's not a forgotten lunch box, it's lost gym clothes. If it's not a bruised knee, it's spilled Cheerios. If it's not nightmares, it's temper tantrums. Truly, it's always something.

Motherhood is never what we predicted, and yet, somehow, we are still surprised every time something doesn't go according to plan.

In addition to the everyday disruptions that can challenge even the most organized of moms, our lives are also rerouted by more significant circumstances. From navigating special needs to loving rebellious teens, we adjust our expectations for motherhood again and again.

These are not experiences unique to the moms in my church. All mothers have had days and years that looked nothing like they planned.

Perhaps better than most, Jesus's mother, Mary, knew the unexpected upheavals of motherhood (see chap. 4). She was an unmarried virgin when an angel appeared and announced her pregnancy, and her life as a mom didn't get any more predictable from there. Soon after Jesus's birth, motherhood put Mary's life in danger and forced her to emigrate to a foreign country (Matt. 2:13–15). Later, she searched for three anxious days for her preteen, who'd been in the temple all along (Luke 2:41–51). Over the course of thirty years, she pondered the mystery of her son's identity (Luke 2:19, 51), witnessed his miracles (John 2:1–12), and reckoned with her place as just one mother among many in her son's eternal family (Matt. 12:46–50).

Motherhood was nothing Mary could have anticipated.

In the final hours of Jesus's earthly life, Mary experienced the greatest sorrow of motherhood. She stood at the cross as soldiers gambled for her son's clothing and the grave waited for his life.

But in the hour of her son's death, she was not abandoned: "When Jesus saw his mother and the disciple whom he loved standing nearby, he said to his mother, 'Woman, behold your son!' Then he said to the disciple, 'Behold your mother!'" (John 19:26–27). From the cross, Jesus took notice of her and cared for her. At the worst moment of her motherhood, he provided a family and a future for her.

Dear sister, this same Jesus cares for you in the struggles of your own motherhood. When upheavals overtake you and you stand, helpless, at the foot of his cross, he will show you the same tender care he showed Mary. He will give you a family in his church and a future in his heavenly kingdom. What's more, he will give you his very self—broken for your sins and raised for your new life.

In the pages of this book, Katie Faris will point you again and again to the precious promises of Scripture for struggling moms. She'll show you that it's okay to weep at the cross for the sorrows motherhood has brought you, but then she'll lift your eyes to the Savior who suffered on the cross for you. As you experience the unexpected, she'll remind you that in Jesus Christ we have a faithful friend and a Savior for sinners. He is the "sure and steadfast anchor of the soul" (Heb. 6:19), and in him we have the hope and comfort we need.

Introduction

IF YOU'RE READING THIS BOOK, it's likely motherhood looks different than you expected. Maybe something you hoped for is missing, or maybe you face challenges you never saw coming. Or you want to help someone for whom that's the case. My prayer is that this book offers gospel hope and comfort to all moms, but especially to those who feel hurt and bewildered by the unexpected sorrows of motherhood. But first, a memory.

A Story of Suffering and Grace

I sat at the kitchen table, a teenager in animated conversation with my mom, when she paused. A fleeting look passed over her eyes, and I tried to discern its meaning. Now it makes more sense; that moment was an awakening. As her mind traced back over the years, my mom realized something: *I didn't remember.*

While you and I live the more painful parts of motherhood, a lot of times our children are oblivious. They don't know anything different than what they experience. At least in the beginning, their suffering is simply part of their experience. It could be elevated liver enzymes or a missing limb. Like the milk they drink or the sunlight passing warmth over their faces, it just is. For me, learning to crawl in a back brace had simply been learning to crawl. As a child, I hadn't thought twice about the fact that I looked like a turtle lugging its shell. It's just the way it was.

That afternoon, it clicked for my mom. I didn't remember things that for her were so vivid and packed with emotion: all the dire pronouncements from doctors; dozens of X-rays; challenges surrounding finding a specialist; financial concerns; and prayers of caring family and friends. I'd forgotten all of them along with my first taste of rice cereal.

But my mom remembered so much, from my arrival at dawn and first smile to the deep concern over my mixed-up vertebrae, the diagnosis of congenital kyphoscoliosis, and the questions about what the future would look like for her baby who wasn't like other babies. She knew the agony and tears that came with simultaneously loving the little girl God had specially formed while fighting the perception that motherhood hadn't delivered a well-formed daughter. And she understood how God had used that same agony and those same tears to deepen the roots of what had been her newly found faith and plant her in the soil of his word. With strong threads, the Lord had woven together the hearts of a young father, a new mother, and their firstborn child—a family—and had fused the bonds between this family and their church family, who joined them in praying and watching how God would work.

That day in the kitchen, my mom told me a story of suffering and grace, of pain and praise, of sacrifice and surrender, of hope and comfort. It was a story that neither she nor I chose, but it was a story in which God was the hero.

Hope and Comfort for You

What's your story, and who are its main characters? How has motherhood been a source of heartache or confusion, and when has it kept you awake at night? What plot twists have you already navigated, and what challenges do you currently face? Which chapters of your story prompt you to question God's goodness and how it plays out in your life? Whoever you are, and whatever your story is, thank you for opening *God Is Still Good: Gospel Hope and Comfort for the Unexpected Sorrows of Motherhood*.

Decades have passed since that conversation with my mom, and I've learned for myself that motherhood is much more than suffering, but it's not less, and there's a particular kind of suffering that moms experience. Maybe you've been walking on a difficult path for a long time, or maybe you're just starting out. Not to discourage you, but if you haven't encountered any thorns on your motherhood journey yet, you probably will at some point. When you do, in this book I hope you hear the validation of your pain. Whether you and I endure hardship in our own bodies or as moms caring for children facing difficulties, our afflictions are real, and our pain is worthy of grief.

But that's not all. While the Lord may not answer all our questions about our trials, the Bible provides a framework that explains our suffering and helps us combat common temptations and lies that travel with them. Through his word, God offers real hope and comfort even for the most heart-wrenching parts of motherhood. This hope is more than wishful thinking because it is grounded in God's past, present, and future faithfulness and anchored in the gospel of Jesus Christ. Similarly,

God's comfort is more than sympathy—it offers courage and strength to the afflicted.

Yes, God is still good.

I may not know your name, but the Lord does. As you read, I pray that he uses the truths in this book to reassure you of his goodness toward you. God has given us stories of suffering and grace, and whether we tell them to our children at a kitchen table one day or to the ladies in our small groups or to an even broader audience, may they reflect his story and bring him much glory.

1

Motherhood Isn't What I Expected

MOTHERHOOD ISN'T WHAT I EXPECTED. It hasn't delivered all that I hoped it would, and instead it's given me some things I never asked for. What about you? Has motherhood been all you dreamed it would be? If not, you aren't as alone as you might think.

To be honest, I'm not sure what I expected. But it's been a whole lot more—more joy and more sorrow. It's also been both; it's been a call to service and sacrifice as well as one of the most rewarding experiences imaginable under heaven. While being a mom is a desirable and godly calling, it's one that exposes a heart to the wounding arrows of pain and grief. Some say it's a labor of love; it's also labor *and* love.

Keep in mind, there's no one-size-fits-all. Sometimes motherhood blooms in the security of a loving marriage, but sometimes a baby is born into a strained marriage or outside of marriage altogether. Motherhood can come according to plan, sooner or later than hoped, or only briefly, leaving us empty-armed and soul-scarred. It arrives by Caesarean section, vaginal delivery, foster care, or adoption; to poverty or financial stability; with ecstasy or trauma.

We moms aren't one-size-fits-all either. We bring a variety of ages, ethnicities, family backgrounds, educational and career choices, life experiences, and expectations with us on this both wonderful and perilous journey. All these factors impact how we approach and process the wins and losses of mom life—wins and losses which are themselves both real and varied.

So when we traverse this road called motherhood and approach the vulnerable places where it meets suffering, we do so bearing burdens of all shapes and sizes. Similarly, our detours onto more precarious paths may differ significantly. One mom encounters the sign with an arrow pointing to "Infertility" while another reads "Special Needs." Some approach these signs earlier on their parenting journey; others bump into "Childhood Leukemia" or "Rebellious Daughter" further down the road. Sadly, some moms expect to read "Racial Discrimination"; others, like me, are surprised by "Genetic Condition."

Each of our stories is unique, but all matter. Each mother and each child is an image bearer of immense value and worth in the eyes of Almighty God, and though gut-wrenching and tear-stained, our stories find meaning and redemption when they are viewed as part of his story.

We can feel isolated on these thorny, off-road trails of motherhood. Whether alone in the NICU, a bedroom, or a food pantry line, we can be cut off from or misunderstood by family and friends. But these paths can also be the very same places where we meet Jesus for the first time—or get to know him and his ways better. Jesus is the God-man: "Though he was in the form of God, [he] did not count equality with God a thing to be grasped, but emptied himself, by taking the form of a servant, being born in the likeness of men" (Phil. 2:6–7).

As one who understands the human experience, and suffering in particular, Jesus sympathizes with our weaknesses. And even though he resisted temptation, he knows its pull. We can expect grace and help when we draw near to Jesus on these lonely paths (Heb. 4:15–16).

Whether it's stretch marks, late-night feedings, a child's compromised immune system, or a wayward teenager, there are real hardships that accompany this beautiful calling. Motherhood may require more faith than anything else we've ever participated in, but it can also open our eyes much wider to our complete dependence on Jesus, his sufficiency, the beauty of the gospel, and the soul-satisfying promises of God. Stressed, weary, hurting, anxious, fearful, and struggling moms like you and me are desperate for the hope and comfort that God offers in his word when motherhood doesn't deliver as expected. Here's some of my story.

Growing Up

One of my favorite children's book series was The Boxcar Children by Gertrude Chandler Warner. As the oldest child in my family, I think I admired the self-sufficiency of the four main characters and how they looked out for one another after their parents died. Later, I devoured *Anne of Green Gables*, L. M. Montgomery's story of an imaginative orphan girl who finds an unlikely but loving home with an elderly brother and sister. (I'm not sure how my parents felt about my attraction to orphan tales, but my mom and dad supported my love for reading.) Perhaps influenced by this steady literary diet, when I thought of being a mom in my early years, my mental image included adopting at least six children. There was no husband in those early aspirations toward motherhood.

At some point in adolescence, my ideas shifted. Boys became more interesting—intriguing, actually. I thought I might even want to kiss one. My physical and emotional maturity coincided with a spiritual awakening. No longer the want-to-be self-sufficient child imagining herself as a strong, self-sufficient single woman raising a boatload of kids, my thoughts expanded, leaving more room for marriage. They also became more rooted in Scripture.

Having been brought up in a Christian home, I knew the gospel and trusted in Jesus for the forgiveness of my sins at an early age. But in my teen years, I wrestled to make my faith my own. As the Lord met me in that struggle, my love for the Bible also grew. Reading that Eve was designed as a helper for Adam, equally addressed in God's mandate, "'Be fruitful and multiply and fill the earth and subdue it'" (Gen. 1:28), I began to wonder whether God might have a husband for me, someone with whom I would be united in work and mission. I started contemplating the future from the perspective of helper, nurturer, and caregiver. My much younger brother and sister as well as extensive babysitting opportunities outside of my home gave me plenty of practical experience caring for children during my teen years.

Even as I pursued a college education and then ministry opportunities, desires for marriage and motherhood were strong, and I regularly prayed for the man I hoped to marry and any children we would have.

Not What I Expected

For me, marriage and children came later than I expected, but they came fairly close together. Before I married Scott Faris—my tall, handsome, wise, humble, funny, gifted, and faith-filled husband—we talked about how many children we might have, Lord willing. I was twenty-seven and he was thirty-five, and we decided that if we wanted to have three or four children, we should start our family sooner rather than later.

On our wedding day, Scott's dad (who is a pastor) prayed for our future children in front of friends and family. A month and a half later, I sat on our queen-sized bed in a bright, sunny apartment bedroom holding a positive pregnancy test. In shock, I showed it to my new husband, feeling guilty for my tears and wanting faith to embrace this desired but unexpectedly early gift of our first child.

It didn't take long for the wonder surrounding this new baby growing in my womb to overcome my trepidation, and soon I had a stack of prenatal books next to that bed, telling me what to expect in labor and delivery and as a new mom. I read the websites too, the ones that compared the size of my developing child to a blueberry or an avocado.

For some reason, though, I skipped all the sections explaining what to expect in the event of a Cesarean delivery. Maybe I didn't think they applied to me—there was no family history to suggest that they would. When my firstborn was frank breech (sitting upright instead of head down) and his amniotic fluid was low at six days past my due date, I faced an emergency C-section. That was the first of many surprises, and perhaps it was my first detour off the road of motherhood that I had expected to follow.

Then came the feeding challenges and the bottles that over-flowed our kitchen sink; the time demands of breastfeeding, pumping milk, and supplementing with formula; and the painful details of realizing two months into mom life that my son was tongue-tied and needed a surgical procedure to help him suck more efficiently. In the meantime, my incision took weeks to heal, and it was months before I felt comfortable in my body and clothes again. The books hadn't prepared me for any of it. Suffice it to say, as much as I loved my newborn and being his mom, motherhood didn't look or feel the way I'd anticipated.

It isn't wrong to imagine and look forward to rocking and cuddling a new baby, but most of my early memories as a mom were anything but serene and relaxed. I grieved the absence of something I had hoped for—an elusive, unhurried bonding that didn't involve problem-solving and tears, midnight walks down the hallway, and fears pounding loudly in my mind as I tried in vain to console my infant son. I was in the middle of my first personal encounter with motherhood, and my reality didn't line up with my expectations.

What I Didn't Expect

As in my experience with a newborn, sometimes motherhood doesn't deliver what we had hoped for. Other times, it bears something we didn't expect.

Before I was a mom, I didn't care what color eyes or hair my baby would have. I wanted the gender to be a surprise. And since my husband and I were committed to loving and caring for our child no matter what, we decided not to do any extra genetic testing prior to birth.

But then came a time when genes suddenly mattered. By the summer of 2013 Scott and I had four children, an infant baby girl and her three older brothers ages two, five, and seven. Our hearts and hands were full. We'd weathered tantrums and tumbles, mosquito bites and bee stings, crumbs and black Sharpie marks on our couch. But we hadn't seen this one coming.

Following a concerning illness, one child was diagnosed with a serious genetic condition called Alpha-1 Antitrypsin Deficiency (Alpha-1) that can have life-threatening impacts on the liver in childhood and the liver or lungs over time. On a bright summer day, Scott and I learned that two more of our children also had this condition. Already reeling from one child's diagnosis, we were devastated. In that moment, I asked what my mother had asked when she heard my diagnosis, and what so many other moms have asked: "Why couldn't it have been me instead? Why my *children*?"

Scott and I huddled together on our front porch, weeping. We cried for our children, for ourselves, for all of it—pain, sorrow, sin, the fall, broken bodies, and messed-up genes. I sobbed until my abs hurt because of that inconsolable ache inside my gut that things weren't as I thought they should be, and I couldn't do anything about it. I knew "all things work together for good" for God's children (Rom. 8:28), but what good could come from any of this? In my sorrow, did I still believe God really was good—and that what he does is good, and for good?

Hope and Comfort for Moms in All Seasons and Stages

I don't live in that place of desperate grief right now, eyes red and swollen from weeping, but I remember it well, and I walk with a painful awareness that I might relive it at any moment. The years since that time have included pediatric specialists, additional diagnoses, diet changes, ambulance rides, finger pricks, hospital stays, and repeated blood draws. My husband and I are on a first-name basis with our pharmacists, and our family's medications regularly fill the drawer labeled *F* (for "Faris") behind the counter. We've battled the flu, pneumonia, and COVID-19 along with perplexity, anxiety, fear, and loneliness surrounding our children's conditions. And I've faced disappointment, not in my children or motherhood itself, both of which I view as gifts, but in the ambiguous loss of some kind of "normal" childhood without the sting of these add-ons.

I don't know what this journey called motherhood has looked like for you, where you've walked on a broad, well-traveled, and familiar road or where your experience has taken you off-road, following unexpected trails. But if you've walked some of the more harrowing paths of motherhood, I want to assure you that no matter how lonely you feel, you're not alone.

You're in good company. While your story and experience are unique, there are moms who have walked precarious paths before you. There are moms facing similar challenges today—moms like me who sometimes feel our foothold slipping and who are attuned to anticipate something lurking, ready to pounce, when we round the next bend. The apostle Peter reminded persecuted Christians that "the same kinds of suffering are being experienced by your brotherhood throughout the world" (1 Pet. 5:9). Though our suffering, yours and mine, is of a different nature than that of his immediate audience, here's a similar truth: there are women in our neighborhoods, sisters in our churches, and moms around the world experiencing hardships related to suffering and motherhood just like we are. You're not the only one.

And here's another truth that is even more precious: Jesus is a Savior who is familiar with sorrow and "acquainted with grief" (Isa. 53:3). He wants to walk with us—and he is able to help us persevere by faith, with grace—even on difficult paths we never would have chosen. When we walk with the Lord, these off-road trails aren't ends in themselves. They aren't just painful parts of our motherhood journey. They too are part of our journey heavenward. This reality offers great hope and comfort to moms facing challenges in all seasons and stages of motherhood.

The path of a medically complex family wasn't one that my husband and I wandered down on purpose, and this story isn't the one I would've chosen to tell; the telling itself stirs emotions, draws forth tears, and exposes my weaknesses for any and all to know. But "blessed be the God and Father of our Lord Jesus Christ, the Father of mercies and God of all comfort, who comforts us in all our affliction" (2 Cor. 1:3–4). My family's trial is real, but so is God's comfort, and I love him more and cling to him more tightly because of it. My hope is fixed on him, and through it all I can say with certainty that he is still good.

God's Word Speaks to Suffering Moms

While my children's specialists are extremely knowledgeable and some medications are helpful, I don't put my ultimate hope in doctors or treatments to cure my kids. The only true hope I've found is in God's word—which was written "that through endurance and through the encouragement of the Scriptures we might have hope" (Rom. 15:4). In the following chapters, we will explore biblical truths and hear what they say to mothers like us in our sorrow.

One of the beauties of God's word is its relevance for all people and situations, time periods, and cultures. It transcends breast-feeding and bottle-feeding preferences, educational choices, the lines drawn around neighborhoods, and the current political climate. It speaks to all moms of all skin colors who function in all tax brackets. The younger moms and the older ones. The moms who go to an office and those who stay home. The moms whose children need special instruction and those with honors students. It levels the playing field and at the same time raises the bar.

God's word speaks to all of us, telling us that the pain we experience in labor and delivery—or the adoption process—is only a foretaste of the particular suffering a mother endures. Within the Bible's pages, we discover truth that is sufficient to explain our suffering as moms and sustain us in it, even when our contexts vary. The Bible assures believing mothers that our pain isn't in vain and we won't always suffer. No matter how confusing the middle parts of our stories seem, no matter how bitter they taste, we look forward to a very good ending. No matter how tangled and rocky, tear-filled and, yes, even bloody, these paths may be, they lead to a glorious place.

Motherhood may look different than you or I expected, either because we don't have what we hoped for or we have what we didn't see coming. It's more—more joy and more pain. It's both— labor and love, grief and hope. But Christian motherhood is by faith, a faith that sees a trustworthy God weaving our stories, the so-much-more along with the happy and sad parts, into his story of grace and glory.

Prayer

Dear Lord, your ways are higher than ours and your thoughts than ours (Isa. 55:9). Even when we're surprised by our circumstances, you're not. Our wins, our losses—you don't measure them the way we do. We confess that motherhood is more than we expected—more joy and more sorrow. It's both a privilege and a call to sacrifice. Where suffering intersects with this worthy calling, please comfort us and fill our hearts with hope. Give us eyes of faith that see you weaving our stories into your own story. In Jesus's name, amen.

Bible Verses

Isa. 53:3   Phil. 2:6–7

Rom. 15:4   Heb. 4:15–16

2 Cor. 1:3–4   1 Pet. 5:9

Reflection Questions

1. Think about your personal history and how it impacts the way you approach and process the wins and losses of motherhood. What extra baggage do you carry on your parenting journey?

2. Have you encountered any detour signs off the main road of motherhood? If so, which ones? Are you walking any of these off-road trails right now?

3. How does Jesus's humility encourage you in your weakness (Phil. 2:6–7; Heb. 4:15–16)?

4. How have you already experienced comfort in your trials associated with motherhood?

5. To what extent can you see God's goodness in your present circumstances, and where is it hard to find?

2

Real Pain, Real Comfort

HAVE YOU EVER NOTICED how our instincts as women to nurture and serve others—which are good and right—can keep us so task-oriented that sometimes we fail to slow down and process our own internal heart struggles? This is especially true in difficult seasons of motherhood. But some situations stop us in our tracks, and that's what happened to me in the fall of 2018.

In the five years since our children's diagnosis with Alpha-1, their medical picture had grown increasingly complicated. During that time, the Lord added a fifth child to our family, a daughter. Then in the spring before the story I'm about to tell, I lost a baby in miscarriage. In September, when one child's lab results were abnormal, the intensity of my emotional response caught me off guard. Even though my child's blood cell counts normalized within a week or two, that situation revealed an inner turmoil I needed to address.

On a crisp autumn evening, my husband and I went to our friends Andrew and Christina for counsel. As this wise couple asked thoughtful, caring questions, they drew Scott and me out about the challenges in front of us and how we were doing. After listening patiently, Christina said, "Katie, I think you have more grieving to do."

It wasn't what I expected her to say, but she was exactly right, and she helped me understand what I hadn't understood on my own. My miscarriage had landed me in the hospital emergency room where I received a blood transfusion due to extreme blood loss. Between an extended recovery period and the ongoing demands of caring for five children, I had limited time to grieve my immediate loss. But my pain went back even further. For years, unintentionally, I'd buried questions and feelings related to my children under my daily childcare responsibilities. With so many other needs presenting themselves as urgent, grief had taken a backseat.

That night the Lord used my friends to show me that my fluctuating emotions and strong responses were related to real pain that really hurt, and I needed to take time to grieve. My miscarriage, the loss of a little person I had never met, had involved death so close—inside of me. And its hurt illuminated my fierce love and heavy concern I carried daily for my living children. The more recent, wacky lab numbers represented something much bigger, something I couldn't control. They pointed to a deeper heartache and brokenness, sickness and disease, an unknown future, and my fear of more unexpected, premature losses.

Andrew and Christina also pointed me to our shared Savior, the one who was humbled so we could be healed (Isa. 53:5) and who offers mercy and grace in our times of need (Heb. 4:16). They spoke truths about our heavenly Father's love that kept me from falling further down a slippery slope on my off-road trail of mom life.

As they graciously assisted me, in this chapter I want to come alongside you—to help you acknowledge your pain and direct you toward the comfort God supplies.

Acknowledge the Pain

We moms can be hyperaware of the challenges our children face. We can be faithful to pray for them and even to ask others to pray for them. But we still might not realize how deeply our children's pain impacts us. However, acknowledging how suffering related to motherhood touches us personally is often an important step toward experiencing God's comfort in the tender spaces of our hearts. When we recognize our trials for what they are and call out for God's help in them, we find that while affliction is real, God's comfort is real too.

Maybe a family member told you that your hard circumstance isn't so bad, or that it's all in your head, suggesting that you just need to get over it and move on. It's possible a well-meaning friend tried offering solutions to make a difficult situation better when what you needed first was for her to sympathize and say, "I'm so very sorry." You could be the woman who looks around at her friends and secretly feels discouraged because their challenges seem more difficult and they seem so strong, and yet you feel stuck in your trial. Or maybe you've been ignoring a hardship, hoping it will go away, not recognizing the toll it's taking on you and your family.

Sisters, whatever you've been told and whatever you've been telling yourself, I want you to hear the validation of your trial and pain: your affliction is real. I don't know what your specific hardships are, but whether or not you or I expected it when we signed on to parenting, suffering is a guaranteed companion on this road. Since the fall, women have experienced pain related to childbearing (Gen. 3:16).

Some trials are weightier than others. Some are temporary, and others won't go away until heaven. Some are the consequences, direct or indirect, of our own sin; some are the consequences of others' sins against us; and some seem to have no rhyme or reason at all. Nevertheless, every kind of suffering that you or I experience is causally related to the arrival and impact of sin in our fallen world (Rom. 8:20–23), including:

Your sadness as you walk the halls with empty arms.

Your concern as you toss in bed while waiting for your teenage son to come home.

The wheelchairs, allergy appointments, inhalers, and eyeglasses.

The phone call from the police that there's been an accident.

Your daughter's IEP (Individualized Education Program).

The broken wrist in a ballgame.

Your child's fear of bullying at school.

Your fears for your adult son who can't land a job.

Your postpartum depression.

Your toddler fighting the flu.

Your rebellious child.

And the list goes on.

We mothers experience real effects of living in a sin-torn land. However good our intentions might be, ignoring those trials or denying their reality is a far cry from trusting God in them. Not only does ignoring or denying them hinder the healing process, but it makes us prone to increased temptation to sin and more vulnerable to believing Satan's lies. At the very least, doing so promotes a false sense of self-sufficiency and keeps us blind to our dependence on the Lord and our Christian brothers and sisters. But humbly acknowledging our suffering and pain, coupled with calling out to God, positions us to receive the comfort he offers.

We're Jars of Clay

In writing to the Corinthian church, the apostle Paul reminds believers that "we have this treasure in jars of clay, to show that the surpassing power belongs to God and not to us. We are afflicted in every way, but not crushed; perplexed, but not driven to despair; persecuted, but not forsaken; struck down, but not destroyed" (2 Cor. 4:7–9). But what does it mean to be a jar of clay?

We're made of sinews and flesh, blood and bones, T cells and pituitary glands, progesterone and estrogen. As women, we were designed to carry babies, but even when wombs don't work properly and we can't bear children, God designed us as vessels for his glory. And though we're fearfully and wonderfully made (Ps. 139:14), there's a reason Paul calls Christians mere "jars of clay." When I fill Mason jars with homemade applesauce, my family doesn't get excited about the jars but what's inside of them. We weren't designed to draw attention to ourselves—our capacity or endurance or sufficiency—but to the treasure of Christ living in us, God's all-surpassing power, and the transforming work of the gospel.

As jars of clay, we ought to accept the reality of our condition. It's good for us to admit when we're afflicted, perplexed, persecuted, and struck down. Then we're better postured to show-case God's glory. But in our victim culture, it can be a process to learn how to validate trials without also developing a victim mentality. Let's briefly talk about this before we explore God's comfort available to us in our suffering.

Our Truest Identity

Despite my diagnosis as a newborn with kyphoscoliosis, my parents excelled at protecting me from any kind of victim status associated with my condition. Granted, it was hard to fall asleep wearing my Boston brace, especially on summer nights that were thick with humidity and in a home without central air condition-ing. And the neighborhood kids were overly curious about my extra-thick layer. But overall, I didn't feel sorry for myself, and I was relatively unaware of the fact that other people might feel sorry for me either.

My parents' sorrow surrounding my abnormal back and all of the questions, fears, predictions, and concerns involving my prog-nosis drove them to the Lord. During my infant years, their faith established deep roots in the soil of God's word and its promises for all of life. As a result, they spent more time in personal Bible study, teaching me about Jesus, and taking me to church than they did talking about my condition. So although I was aware of my deformity, it was never a question in my mind where my true identity was found.

I wasn't primarily a victim of my circumstances but rather their beloved daughter whom they had dedicated to the Lord. When I professed faith in Jesus Christ at a young age, I understood that I was a new creation. "Therefore, if anyone is in Christ, he is a new creation. The old has passed away; behold, the new has come" (2 Cor. 5:17). My new identity as God's beloved, adopted daughter was secure.

It's actually been more tempting for me to swing on the pendulum toward victim status in my encounters with suffering as a mom, especially in more medically charged seasons with my children. Nevertheless, the Lord regularly and graciously reminds me that *victim* is not who I am. My suffering is an overwhelmingly painful part of my story, but it's not all of my story. And it certainly doesn't define me or my children.

The same is true for all of us. When we place our hope in Christ's finished work on the cross, our lives are hidden with him (Col. 3:3), we're adopted into his family (Rom. 8:14–17), and one day God himself will be with us as our God (Rev. 21:3–4). This reality means we can acknowledge the challenges of being special needs parents without claiming that label as our primary identity. It's possible to grieve when an adult child renounces his Christian heritage without being defined as a failed parent. There's a time and place to cry out against racial injustice when it impacts our families and at the same time preach to ourselves and our children that we belong to a heavenly King who vindicates his own. Why? Because our suffering doesn't define us; our relationship with our heavenly Father does. We are daughters.

God's Comfort Is Real Too

We don't have to stuff our pain, gloss over it, or prove anything in it. Instead, as daughters we can run to our heavenly Father, "the Father of mercies and God of all comfort, who comforts us in all our affliction" (2 Cor. 1:3–4). In his presence, we can be honest about our struggles and learn what true comfort is.

When Scott and I met with Andrew and Christina, the Lord used our friends to help us identify and acknowledge the deeper pain hidden underneath the surface of our busy lives. That night, Scott and I felt comfortable—familiar and at ease—sitting on our friends' couch, but Scripture talks about a comfort that includes much more than that. Biblical comfort isn't just a soft blanket or a steaming cup of coffee (although I enjoy both on cold winter mornings). When Isaiah writes, "Comfort, comfort my people, says your God," he uses a form of the Hebrew word *nachamu*, which suggests strengthening and giving courage (Isa. 40:1).

Isaiah's message offered a strengthening kind of comfort to his original readers, and his words reassure and encourage moms like us that true, soul-satisfying comfort is found in knowing that in Christ our "warfare is ended" and our iniquities pardoned (Isa. 40:2). As Christians living on the other side of the cross, we understand that this reality is possible only because Jesus suffered on our behalf. When we encounter difficulties and pain, the truth of the gospel is what bolsters and sustains us for the long haul.

Isaiah also invites us to look up and consider the character of the one who offers us abiding comfort:

> Lift up your eyes on high and see:
>   who created these?
> He who brings out their host by number,
>   calling them all by name;

by the greatness of his might
    and because he is strong in power,
    not one is missing. (Isa. 40:26)

In other words, look up at the great God who calls the stars by name and makes sure not one of them falls out of the sky. This is the same God who sees your tears and hears your cries. And guess what? He "does not faint or grow weary" (Isa. 40:28). What's more, "he gives power to the faint, / and to him who has no might he increases strength" (40:29). That's the kind of comfort that our "everlasting God, / the Creator of the ends of the earth" offers to his beloved children (40:28).

God's comfort strengthens and helps us stand firm in our faith through our affliction, not just on the other side of it. This comfort is tied to Jesus Christ, born to be the "consolation of Israel" (Luke 2:25), the one who secured our comfort and through whom we have "strong encouragement to hold fast to the hope set before us. We have this as a sure and steadfast anchor of the soul" (Heb. 6:18–19). And we experience God's comfort today through the ministry of the Holy Spirit, our Comforter (John 14:16, 26; 15:26; 16:7).[1]

As Andrew read Scripture and prayed for Scott, me, and our family that night, the Lord deeply comforted our souls. Recognizing that our difficulties didn't have any easy answers or quick solutions, our friends pointed us to our strong, capable, faithful,

---

1 The Greek word *parakletos* is used in the New Testament to refer to the Holy Spirit. While *parakletos* is often translated as "Advocate" or "Helper," its broader meaning includes "Comforter" and "Counselor" in the sense of coming alongside of someone with aid and assistance.

sovereign, and loving Father who doesn't offer empty platitudes or false assurances but does keep all his promises. This is the kind of comfort you and I need.

Comfort for Hurting and Bewildered Moms

One of the things I love about God's comfort is that while it's very personal, it doesn't end with a single recipient. Paul says God comforts us "so that we may be able to comfort those who are in any affliction, with the comfort with which we ourselves are comforted by God" (2 Cor. 1:4). Andrew and Christina have walked their own challenging road as parents; that's one reason Scott and I chose to go to them when we were struggling. As recipients of God's comfort, they ministered to us out of an overflow of the comfort that God had supplied to them during their own family trials.

Your suffering may look unrecognizable next to mine, but it's just as real and maybe even significantly more painful. But to whatever degree you are afflicted, God's comfort is also real and available. His word is full of truths that offer comfort—the strengthening and encouraging kind—to hurting and bewildered moms. We'll consider many of them in the following pages. And as God comforts you, he also prepares you to comfort others.

Pausing to acknowledge the nature of our struggles and admit their toll on us can be overwhelming, but when we do so prayerfully, God works powerfully to redirect our gaze toward him and his ways. The psalmist wrote, "It is good for me that I was afflicted, / that I might learn your statutes" (Ps. 119:71). And while on our down days we might question the accuracy of this statement, it holds a precious truth: our trials provide opportunities for us to learn things about God and his word that we might not learn any other way. Knowing God as our Comforter and experiencing his comfort in the harder parts of motherhood are some of those things.

Prayer

Dear Lord, we confess our complete dependence on you. Apart from you, we can do nothing; but when we abide in you, we bear much fruit (John 15:5). In our affliction, please multiply your comfort. Strengthen and help us. Encourage and sustain our faith that you are still good through our trials. Make us ministers of your comfort to others, and let us always be jars of clay that show off your glory. In Jesus's name, amen.

Bible Verses

Gen. 3:16

Pss. 119:71; 139:14

Isa. 40:1, 26, 28–29; 53:5

Luke 2:25

John 14:16, 26;
    15:26; 16:7

Rom. 8:20–23

2 Cor. 1:3–4; 4:7–9; 5:17

Col. 3:3

Heb. 4:16; 6:18–19

Rev. 21:3–4

Reflection Questions

1. Have you ever needed help acknowledging a hardship you faced?

2. What does it mean that "every kind of suffering that you or I experience is causally related to the arrival and impact of sin in our fallen world"? Read Romans 8:20–23.

3. What affliction—or afflictions—do you currently face for which you could use God's comfort?

4. Are you cultivating friendships and habits that position you to receive biblical comfort?

5. Is there someone the Lord is bringing to mind whom you could comfort today?

3

Grief-Worthy

NOT ONLY IS OUR PAIN RELATED to the trials of motherhood real, and our confused responses to those trials valid, but our trials are grief-worthy. The afflictions we face as moms—either in our own bodies or as we carry the burden of love and care for our children—include all kinds of losses. Lost sleep, lost time, and lost relationships. Suffering also costs us mental and emotional energy, wearing on our bodies and souls, and it often brings financial burdens. These losses and costs might not all be equal, but we're right to grieve whenever our bodies and our children's bodies don't work the way God originally intended.

Sometimes, even in church, a grieving woman is told, "Get over it." Bible verses are passed out like Band-Aids, or a distressed woman is simply misunderstood. Thankfully, in recent years there has been more conversation in many churches about the role and importance of godly lament as part of the grieving process. Both from personal experience and from conversations with other believers, I agree that while the practice of lament is helpful to the church at large, it is especially beneficial to hurting moms. Instead of ignoring our grief or trying to speed our way through it, godly lament is a vehicle to bring our sadness and disappointment to the Lord. In this chapter, we'll consider the value of godly lament, Hannah's example in practicing it, how we actually do it, and some of its benefits.

The Value of Godly Lament

The *Merriam-Webster* dictionary defines *lament* as "a crying out in grief."[1] When talking about *godly lament*, these passionate cries are directed toward the Lord in prayer. They include wailing and moaning, questions and pleas. This kind of lament agrees with God, saying, "Yes, God, sin really messed everything up. Our world is so broken. We need you, Lord, and we need you to do what only you can do. Turn our ashes into beauty. Redeem our stories. You're our only hope." Godly lament invites hurting moms like us to pour out our hearts with emotional freedom before our heavenly Father (Ps. 62:8), confessing our struggles and doubts about God's goodness as well as our faith that God is our only refuge.

But like many Americans, I tend toward impatience. I'll join the shortest checkout line at the grocery store, stay busy on my phone while waiting in the doctor's office, and have to remind myself to adjust my pace when traveling anywhere with young children. This kind of impatience resists making time for godly lament. I want everything in my life to come quickly, and that includes resolution to my grief. If I'm not tempted to bypass it

---

1 *Merriam-Webster*, s.v. "lament (*n.*)," https://www.merriam-webster.com/dictionary /lament.

altogether, I at least want to move through its awkwardness and discomfort as quickly as possible.

Have you ever tried to sidestep grief and lament on your way to the other side of a difficult situation? Instead of circumventing grief's confusing emotions, the Lord invites us to bring them to him. We don't have to cast a positive spin on something that really stinks. Biblical lament provides a way for us to engage with God at a heart level in our scariest and most gut-wrenching parenting moments.

In Ecclesiastes, the Preacher says, "For everything there is a season, and a time for every matter under heaven" (Eccles. 3:1). In motherhood, there is "a time to weep, and a time to laugh" (3:4)—there are times for both. But while we enjoy lingering in seasons of laughter, it can be harder to embrace our seasons of weeping. Nevertheless, we make time for what we value, and we should both value and make time for lament. Hannah offers a beautiful example of a woman in the Old Testament who did.

Hannah's Example of Godly Lament

Hannah lived in Israel toward the end of the period of the judges and before the land was ruled by kings. Yearly, she would travel with her husband, Elkanah, along with his second wife, Peninnah, and Peninnah's children to Shiloh. There they would worship and offer sacrifices to the Lord (1 Sam. 1:3).

Not only did Hannah experience personal disappointment related to infertility, but in a culture where childbearing was highly prized, she suffered the shame of barrenness and the provocations of her rival. And she didn't leave these challenges at home. They traveled with her to Shiloh.

While her family feasted, Hannah wouldn't eat (1:7). She was undone. She couldn't take it anymore. When her pain was great, she turned to the only one she knew to go to—the Lord. Notice, at least in this example, she didn't rail against her husband or return Peninnah's insults. Instead, when sorrow was added to sorrow and Hannah reached her emotional breaking point, she "prayed to the LORD and wept bitterly" (1:10). Before him, she poured out her heart in words that only he could hear: "O LORD of hosts, if you will indeed look on the affliction of your servant and remember me and not forget your servant, but will give to your servant a son, then I will give him to the LORD all the days of his life" (1:11).

Hannah's pathos was so intense that Eli the priest thought she was drunk (1:14); as if she hadn't experienced enough grief, Eli totally misunderstood and misjudged this deeply wounded woman. But Hannah explained that she wasn't drunk but "troubled in spirit" (1:15). Eli then changed his tune, and the Lord used this imperfect messenger to comfort Hannah with these words: "Go in peace, and the God of Israel grant your petition that you have made to him" (1:17). After her prayer to the Lord and this conversation with Eli, "[She] went her way and ate, and her face was no longer sad" (1:18).

Godly lament produced its intended effect in Hannah. She walked away comforted—strengthened and encouraged—and ready to do the next thing. She rejoined her family and "worshiped before the LORD" before traveling home (1:19). This change alone was evidence of the Lord's grace at work in Hannah's life, but God went a step further: "The LORD remembered her. And in due time Hannah conceived and bore a son, and she called his name Samuel" (1:19–20). After Samuel was weaned, Hannah kept her promise and brought him to serve the Lord at Shiloh.

Hannah's song ends this story, and in it we read some of the truths she learned about God on her difficult motherhood journey. First, she came to understand that there is no one like the Lord (1 Sam. 2:2). What's more, God knows everything, even our motives (2:3). In his sovereignty, he often flips our stories—as Hannah experienced firsthand when God gave her not only Samuel but five additional children (2:4–8, 21). Finally, the Lord guards "his faithful ones" (2:9), and he has complete authority and ultimate control (2:10).

Practicing Godly Lament

When a teacher tells you that your autistic son disrupted the Sunday school class—again—where can you run? When attachment issues surface with an adopted child, where can you turn? When you feel the weight of parenting alone, where can you look? When your own lack of sleep, postpartum depression, or other physical ailment makes parenting that much harder, where can you go? The answer to all of these questions is the same: we can go to God. When Hannah's hopes for motherhood didn't deliver, she ran to God, not away from him. And just as Hannah turned to the Lord in her grief, we can run to him in our sorrows.

Like Hannah, you and I can humble ourselves before God. We find empty chapels in children's hospitals and wail with the doors closed. We take walks in the woods or a quiet neighborhood and turn our questions and anxieties into prayers. We kneel beside our beds at home and cry,

How long, O Lord? Will you forget me forever?
How long will you hide your face from me?

> How long must I take counsel in my soul
> and have sorrow in my heart all the day? (Ps. 13:1–2)

When we bring our sorrows and afflictions to the Lord and express our grief before him in godly lament, he hears our cries just as he heard Hannah's. We find hope and comfort in knowing that God will remember us too—in his time and in his way. We might not get the baby—or the breakthrough or whatever else we're hoping for—as she did. But even though our heavenly Father may or may not answer our desperate prayers the way we desire, one thing is sure: we too will get to know him better. We'll come back to this theme repeatedly in this book.

One thing we learn when we draw near to the Lord in our brokenness is that he is compassionate. David, another go-to example for godly lament, wrote that God "is near to the brokenhearted / and saves the crushed in spirit" (Ps. 34:18). And the author of Lamentations (maybe Jeremiah), who witnessed extreme heartache and wrote an entire book of lament, wrote this:

> For the Lord will not
> cast off forever,
> but, though he cause grief, he will have compassion
> according to the abundance of his steadfast love;
> for he does not afflict from his heart
> or grieve the children of men. (Lam. 3:31–33)

Even in bleak circumstances, these men recognized that their hope was in God and his ultimate tenderness toward his children.

Again, David wrote these words about the Lord when the Philistines seized him:

> You have kept count of my tossings;
>> put my tears in your bottle.
> Are they not in your book? (Ps. 56:8)

This verse contains an evocative word picture, suggesting a depth of loving care we'd hardly expect from Almighty God. Instead of scorning our weakness, he counts every time we toss under our bedsheets, unable to sleep as another day's cares weigh on our minds. Our loving Father, who knows when we sit down and rise up, who "discerns our thoughts from afar" and every word before we speak it (Ps. 139:2), can be trusted with each tear we shed. We learn this truth when we bring our grief to him.

I understand how difficult it can be to make time for grief and lament, especially when our care loads are great. If this is a challenge for you, ask God to show you how to carve out time for this important process. Perhaps your spouse or a friend can help you look at your schedule and set aside a specific time to read God's word and pray about a current or past struggle. In an especially intense season, it might just be taking five minutes to step out of the room, cry, and pray when something triggers your emotions. Talking to a pastor, a professional counselor, or even a friend who has walked a similarly hard road to yours could be hugely helpful in processing your grief and thinking through what godly lament looks like for you in your particular situation. Whatever action the Lord leads you to take, I hope it's clear that your suffering related to motherhood is grief-worthy.

I'm Proof of the Benefits of Godly Lament

In the months following our children's diagnosis of Alpha-1, even if I'd wanted to hide my grief, I don't think I could have. This new normal seemed to touch every aspect of our family's daily life, and grief traveled with it, filling my insides until it seeped out of my pores. Whenever a friend asked how I was doing, I'd cry. Every Sunday at church, moved by a lyric in a song or a Scripture application that fit my circumstances or an affectionate hug from a church member, I'd cry. It was awkward. It was uncomfortable. I probably made some people feel embarrassed. But this opened the door for me to receive prayer and God's compassionate care through believing friends that I otherwise might not have.

In other seasons, though, such as the one following my miscarriage, grief functioned differently. This became apparent the night when Scott and I met with Andrew and Christina, as mentioned in the previous chapter. One decision my friends helped me make was to set aside a designated time to grieve the baby we lost in miscarriage and process my deep sadness. Between homeschooling our older children and navigating their various needs as well as caring for a sixteen-month-old baby, it wasn't easy to carve out time alone, so Scott and I decided that I would join him in traveling to a conference he needed to attend. My parents agreed to care for our children at home; then, while Scott participated in meetings, I could use our hotel room for extended periods of solitude. This would allow me time to think, pray, read, journal, and cry—to exercise godly lament.

I remember how quiet it was when Scott left me alone in that hotel room. I wasn't sure how to begin, what to say or do first. But I opened my Bible and prayed that the Lord would lead me, and that time turned out to be such a gift. While I can't say that it cured my grief, it provided much-needed space to reflect, ask questions, and address some of the enemy's accusations with biblical truth. I wailed, wiped my eyes and nose, and then wailed some more. Between sobs, I told the Lord, "This hurts." Then I invited the Spirit to intercede for me "with groanings too deep for words" (Rom. 8:26).

As I did, the Lord gave me words to process my experience. Here's a slightly edited excerpt taken from my journal from that week:

> In past weeks especially [since our meeting with Andrew and Christina], the Lord has graciously helped me to see and acknowledge his great love for me in the midst of [Scott's and my] miscarriage. Repeatedly, the story of Job has come to mind, reminding me that it wasn't because God didn't love Job that he allowed suffering; but in fact, God commended Job, saying, "There is none like [Job] on the earth, a blameless and upright man" (Job 1:8). God has protected me from the lie that he doesn't love us.
>
> Indeed, he has graciously brought friends and biblical truth to remind me of his continued care and to encourage me to fully grieve and receive his comfort. Head truth and heart feelings sometimes get jumbled, and it's been freeing to let tears flow when needed and to acknowledge the suffering. As much as I'd like to be on the other side, the truth that Jesus himself

"learned obedience through what he suffered" has been helpful to me (Heb. 5:8). I believe the Lord has truth he wants me to learn that can only be learned through suffering, and he has comfort that he is giving that I want to slow down and receive.

Love and Suffering

As Hannah learned truths about God in her suffering, the Lord used godly lament over my miscarriage to help me better comprehend his deep love for his children—for my family in particular. In our lives, as with Job, suffering in no way reflects a change of God's loving heart toward us. But from the beginning, this is the lie that Satan's wily voice has been whispering in our ears: "God doesn't love you." *It's not true—it's simply not true.* God commended Job, whose story we'll consider further in chapter 5, even as he allowed tremendous suffering to touch his life. And no matter what lies you and I are tempted to believe in our suffering, God's love remains constant, and he is good.

John, one of Jesus's twelve disciples, gave details surrounding the death of their friend Lazarus that illustrate this truth. He wrote, "Now Jesus loved Martha and her sister and Lazarus. So, when [Jesus] heard that Lazarus was ill, he stayed two days longer in the place where he was" (John 11:5–6). We know Jesus loved this family because John tells us that he did. Yet he chose to delay, and that decision to linger and move slowly meant that Lazarus was dead—dead and hidden in a tomb that was sealed with a stone—before Jesus and his disciples showed up. It had been long enough for Martha and Mary to give up hope, to put on their mourning clothes and grieve. And it's in this context that we read that famous, shortest verse of the Bible, "Jesus wept" (John 11:35).

Jesus wept. He grieved. Our Savior felt sorrow and loss. He watched his loved ones suffer. As he did, the whole time, he never once stopped loving this family.

The entire time he wept, Jesus knew there was more to their story. He knew a better day was coming. He knew rejoicing was around the corner and God would get glory and Lazarus would rise from the dead. He knew there was a purpose to their pain. And he still took time to weep with his friends. He didn't bulldoze through grief on the way to grace.

In your family's hardships, the Lord hasn't stopped loving you either. He never will. Even if your suffering hurts more tomorrow than it does today, there's more to your story. A better day is coming. Joy is around the corner. God is working his plan, even if you and I don't see it yet. There is purpose to our pain—yours and mine. Yet in the middle of our sorrow, when the tornado of pain touches the ground of our hearts and the storm swirls around us, we're invited to make time for godly lament, just as Jesus did.

The Bible is rich with words of grace and truth that speak to us on our darkest days—the Eeyore days, flat days, down days, and rock-bottom days—but we won't have ears to hear what Scripture says if we don't first recognize the clouds covering our skies, see our need for God and his word, or slow down to listen. However, when we acknowledge our pain and weakness and call our trials "hard" and "scary" and "confusing," and when we take time to engage God in conversation about what's really going on under the surface, we begin to learn the meaning behind these verses in Isaiah:

I will give you the treasures of darkness
   and the hoards in secret places,
that you may know that it is I, the LORD. (Isa. 45:3)

When we run to God with godly lament rather than away from him in our grief, we discover priceless treasures, getting to know him in ways we never knew him before.

Prayer

Dear Lord, in our trials, help us embrace godly lament. Thank you for remembering Hannah in her suffering, and thank you for remembering us in ours. You are a compassionate God, and we bring all our doubts, questions, fears, uncertainties, and tears to you. Even on our darkest days, assure us of your love for us and reveal truths about your character and promises that we couldn't learn any other way. In Jesus's name, amen.

Bible Verses

1 Sam. 1:1–2:10, 21	Isa. 45:3
Job 1:8	Lam. 3:31–33
Pss. 13:1–2; 34:18; 56:8;	John 11:1–44
62:8; 139:2	Rom. 8:26
Eccles. 3:1–4	Heb. 5:8

Reflection Questions

1. What is your understanding of godly lament?

2. When have you tried to bypass grief? What was the impact?

3. In your current season, how could you set aside time to practice godly lament?

4. How could you help a single mom carve out extended time alone with the Lord? Could you make her a meal and/or offer to watch her children for an afternoon to free up some time for her to do that?

5. What are some truths God is teaching you about himself in your suffering?

4

Another Story

MOTHERHOOD INCLUDES MORE than suffering, but that doesn't change the fact that suffering is part of its package. For some of us, it's a big part. And while godly lament invites us to bring our grief to the Lord, the gospel is the only reason we can find hope and comfort when we do.

What is the gospel? It's the good news that Jesus died on the cross to save us from our sin and restore our relationship with God. It's truly wonderful news. But sometimes you and I can wonder: How does this truth relate to the nitty-gritty details of paying the bills, meeting with the school counselor, and asking a spouse to help with carpool? What does it have to do with my children's Alpha-1 or your child's challenges? It has everything to do with them.

God isn't bewildered by our suffering but has determined to enter into it, and he showed us the full extent of his love when "Christ died for our sins" (1 Cor. 15:3). While we might be tempted to relegate this gospel message to some designated religious corner of our thinking, it's meant to transform every area of our lives—including how we interact with the trials of motherhood. On these off-road paths, preaching the gospel regularly to ourselves reminds us why we suffer in the first place, strengthens us with hope for our journeys, and encourages us that we have much to look forward to.

When circumstances scream at us to despair, give up, and lose heart, God's word tells us another story. It provides a context for our suffering that helps moms like you and me make sense of the painful parts of our stories. To help us understand what this means, in this chapter we'll trace the gospel story through the experiences of two famous mothers in the Bible—Eve and Mary. As we do, we'll see that when we walk our own difficult trails, real comfort is found in Jesus, the one who suffered great sorrow in order to bring us real hope.

Eve's Story

The very first verse of the Bible says, "In the beginning, God created the heavens and the earth" (Gen. 1:1). The Creator spoke, and the world we walk and talk and live in was created—but not as we know it. When God made Eve, the first woman, she experienced something that the rest of us never have: a world without sin.

God saw his creation, "and behold, it was very good" (Gen. 1:31). There were no tears, sleepless nights, blood sugar checks, infertility treatments, hearing screenings, allergy appointments, or stillbirths. There were no disobedient or foolish children, no lazy or angry mothers. It was sinless and stainless—beautiful. It's hard to imagine, because that's not the world that we or our children were born into.[1]

---

1 Some of this content first appeared in "Motherhood Is a Call to Suffer (in Hope)," an article I wrote for The Gospel Coalition, November 13, 2020, https://www.thegospelcoalition.org/.

"God planted a garden in Eden" where Eve lived with her husband, Adam (Gen. 2:8). We don't know how long this garden remained pristine before Eve believed Satan's lies, before she and her husband tasted and swallowed the fruit that infected our human race (3:1–8). But sin spoiled everything and, instead of eternal life, the seeds of death sprouted inside our forebears. Their sin separated them from God, and he drove them out of the garden where they had previously enjoyed sweet fellowship with him.

What's more, God didn't mince words with Eve: "I will surely multiply your pain in childbearing; / in pain you shall bring forth children" (Gen. 3:16). For Eve, this pain would entail more than the sweat and blood and painful contractions involved in labor and delivery. It would include the heartache of knowing one of her sons (Cain) murdered her other son (Abel).

But even on that fateful day when sin seemed to win in the garden, God promised Eve—and us, by extension, as her descendants—that sin wouldn't always hold sway, evil wouldn't always run rampant, and the curse wouldn't always control outcomes. In cursing the serpent, the Lord said:

> I will put enmity between you and the woman,
>   and between your offspring and her offspring;
> he shall bruise your head,
>   and you shall bruise his heel. (Gen. 3:15)

In the pattern of much of the Old Testament, this verse pointed to a present and future fulfillment. It was a prophetic promise that one day Jesus would once and for all crush the head of our true enemy, Satan. But for Eve, that day was a long way off.

Eve's Story Informs Our Stories

Eve's story explains why each mother living on this side of Eden feels the impact and weight of parenting in a confused, hurting, sorrowful, and sin-torn land—one that affects each mother and child. But it's not just that we live in a sinful world and that our own hearts are sinful, though both are true. As Eve's daughters, mothers are stricken by the curse, and the consequences of sin play out in a particular way that's specific to the mother-child relationship. Whether it's laboring through contractions or the adoption process, adding children to our families is agonizing—not to mention the pain we feel when those processes fail us. And raising our children isn't any easier.

This doesn't mean that suffering is always the direct consequence of a particular sin. It's not. For example, the blind man who encountered Jesus didn't suffer because his parents sinned, "but that the works of God might be displayed in him" (John 9:3). Nevertheless, as mentioned already in this book, the suffering you and I experience as moms is causally related to the arrival and impact of sin in our world (Rom. 8:20–23). So what *does* this mean?

It means that the woman whose child just received an unwanted diagnosis feels the effects of the fall. So does the mom with postpartum depression as she struggles to care for her baby; the foster mom consoling a toddler who's afraid of the dark; the mother who juggles feeding challenges, special diets, or allergy appointments; the woman who isn't sure if she can have any more children; the mom who doesn't know how to reach her distant teenager; the grandmother who grieves for her wayward grandchildren; the mother of the addict, the sexually confused, or the depressed; and the aging mom who feels taken advantage of or neglected by her older children. Whenever you or I experience sorrow, disappointment, or frustration because motherhood hasn't played out—or panned out—the way we wanted, hoped, or dreamed, we can trace our struggle back to the garden.

How does knowing the widespread effects of the fall help moms? Even if we don't like it, there's a first cause—a reason—for our pain. There's comfort in knowing God's word doesn't ignore or deny the reality of suffering. Instead, it validates a mother's plight: because of the fall, moms suffer.

Next, rather than my hardship or yours functioning as isolated stories, they are part of another story that unites all moms: the single and the married ones; the stay-at-home and the working ones; moms of all colors and ethnicities; the grieving, frightened, and confused moms. All of us experience pain in childbirth and child-rearing.

But the story of the Bible does more than unite us in suffering; it offers hope to all of us. God promised Eve that one day her offspring would bruise the head of the serpent (Gen. 3:15), and these words spoke comfort and hope to our distant matriarch even as she walked out of Eden. They offer the same encouragement to us. Even though hardship is a given in this life, it doesn't have to be the end of your story or mine because it's not the end of God's. His story is one of promise and redemption, and Mary's story helps us see this more.

Mary's Story

The Bible doesn't tell us what Mary, the mother of Jesus, was doing the day the angel Gabriel appeared to her in Galilee and announced that she would be with child (Luke 1:26–31). She probably wasn't looking to be a character in a story. But through Gabriel's message, her heavenly Father invited her to be part of the most significant story of all time, the story of all stories.

Like us, Mary had been born into a fallen world that desperately needed a Savior. As a young Jewish woman living under Roman rule, she waited expectantly for God to send his promised Messiah. Into this reality, her child was to arrive and be named "'Jesus, for he will save his people from their sins'" (Matt. 1:21).

While birthed by Mary, her child would "be called holy—the Son of God" (Luke 1:35). And while Mary was favored by God with the blessing of carrying this special baby (1:28), this favor was extended to her as a gracious gift—not by her own merits—and was one she received with faith. Unlike Eve who said *no* to God when she entertained Satan and his lies, Mary said *yes* to God's will when she answered Gabriel: "'Behold, I am the servant of the Lord; let it be to me according to your word'" (1:38).

Mary's experience of God's grace led her to compose a song of praise that was remarkably similar to Hannah's (Luke 1:46–55; 1 Sam. 2:1–10). Mary's song magnified the Lord for what he had done for her personally and for believers generally. In it, she notably rejoiced in God as her Savior (Luke 1:47) and proclaimed what she had learned about his character and deeds. She declared him to be mighty and holy (1:49), merciful (1:50), and strong (1:51). She told how he "scattered the proud" (1:51), exalted the humble (1:52), "filled the hungry" (1:53), helped Israel (1:54), and "in remembrance of his mercy," kept his promises (1:54–55).

Mary was given an intimate role as mother of the Son of God, and as such, she witnessed grace and glory along with feeling unimaginable grief and sorrow. In her heart, she treasured and pondered all the shepherds told her, and experienced "a sword [piercing] through [her] own soul also" (Luke 2:19, 35). As a mom, she likely experienced intense emotions when she fled to Egypt to protect her child's life (Matt. 2:13–14), searched for him in Jerusalem (Luke 2:45), watched him change water into wine at the wedding in Cana (John 2:1–12), and witnessed his final breaths and heard his final words as he died on the cross (John 19:25). Through it all, it's reasonable to assume Mary came to know Jesus not only as her son, but as her Savior—the one who died for her sin.

These Stories Point to Jesus

Both Eve's and Mary's stories point to Jesus, and as women who taste from deep wells of both joy and sorrow associated with the calling of motherhood as they did, you and I are invited to see our stories through the lens of his as well. This is really good news. Why? Because our greatest problem isn't what motherhood hasn't delivered, even though it might often feel that way.

Just as it was for Eve and Mary, God's word tells us that our greatest problem is our sin. Paul wrote this in Romans: "For all have sinned and fall short of the glory of God" and "the wages of sin is death" (3:23; 6:23). The seed of sin produces death in our hearts, just as it did in Eve's. The Bible also identifies our greatest needs—for forgiveness, rescue, and salvation from our sin and reconciliation with God. And our only hope of deliverance is found in Jesus, the promised Savior, conceived by the Holy Spirit and born of Mary. Jesus bore our sins on the cross and died in our place. But the tomb wasn't the end. Three days after his burial, Jesus rose to life, showing his power over sin and death and forever bruising the enemy's head. Because of his victory over sin that day, we have hope of salvation: "If you confess with your mouth that Jesus is Lord and believe in your heart that God raised him from the dead, you will be saved" (Rom. 10:9). When we trust in Jesus as our Savior, what begins as redemption of our souls spreads, bringing hope and comfort to the broken and hurting places in our lives. This is the gospel message we ought to preach to ourselves regularly.

But especially in more intense trials or seasons of motherhood, the challenges are not only overwhelming. They're consuming. They involve round-the-clock care and weighty decisions. It's only natural to see the upcoming procedure or a child's rebellious behavior as the greatest problem—and sometimes there's no easy answer or any positive outcome.

Nevertheless, these harsh realities are the effects of living in a sin-infected world, and only one has the power to conquer sin itself. Only one can say, "Your sins are forgiven" (Mark 2:5). Only one defeated death and can rescue us from its clutches. Only one offers hope when the prognosis is hopeless. Only one offers comfort to our broken hearts. Only Jesus, the one who carried our sin to the cross and suffered on our behalf, offers the lasting hope and comfort we need, not only for our difficult moments but for all eternity. This is why we need to remind ourselves of the gospel—in the hardest seasons, most of all.

When our paths are thorny, you and I can know the one who wore a crown of thorns. Jesus walked the road to Calvary, and he is ready to walk with us on our difficult roads. He is faithful and true (Rev. 19:11), and he won't leave us stranded. Instead, he urges us on, reminding us that there's more to these stories.

There's More to These Stories

Eve and Mary both died, but they died with hope that there was more—for them—to God's grand story. How do we, living thousands of years later, hold on to the same hope? We know that future hope doesn't erase past hurt or even promise that we won't be hurt again in this life. We understand the fragility of life and that the motherhood calling makes us vulnerable to a variety of forms of pain and wounding. Miscarriages still happen, and abnormal lab results provoke emotions because they point to underlying conditions, reminding us that any routine test could suddenly signal concern. There's no guarantee that a child will live to adulthood or that brothers and sisters who were brought up together in the faith will all follow Jesus. We still wonder why God allows suffering to hurt our children and inhabit our homes. And, if Jesus really won a decisive victory over sin on the cross so long ago, why do we continue to experience its horrific impacts on our lives? How can we know that God is good in the face of so much suffering?

Our world is still shattered and aching, and our trials are real and painful, but they shouldn't surprise us. Jesus told his disciples, "In the world you will have tribulation. But take heart; I have overcome the world" (John 16:33). We will have trouble, but victory in our war with sin is sure because Jesus has already won the greatest battle. Because of this, there are ways that God can use our trials for good—even today; we'll consider this further in chapter 7. But for now, I want us to cast our eyes farther down the road. Our Lord promises to return, and as we wait for him and the consummation of his eternal, heavenly kingdom on an unknown-to-mankind but determined-by-God future day, we wait with this assurance: we won't always suffer.

In the meantime, our cabinets may be stocked with inhalers, medications, and nutritional supplements; our children still fall down and scrape their knees; we navigate conflicts with our teens; and empty arms hang limp. But that's not the end of our stories because it's not the end of God's. We can't return to Eden, but we have much to look forward to in heaven:

> And I heard a loud voice from the throne saying, "Behold, the dwelling place of God is with man. He will dwell with them, and they will be his people, and God himself will be with them as their God. He will wipe away every tear from their eyes, and death shall be no more, neither shall there be mourning nor crying nor pain anymore, for the former things have passed away."
>
> And he who was seated on the throne said, "Behold, I am making all things new." . . . "Write this down, for these words are trustworthy and true." (Rev. 21:3–5)

One day, we won't feel isolated or separated anymore because God will dwell with us, and we will be with him, face-to-face (1 Cor. 13:12). One day, there will be no more tears, no more death, no more mourning or crying or pain. That also means no more runaways or depression, no more custody battles or difficult parent-teacher conferences, and no more need for blood draws, hospital stays, or wheelchairs. Instead, all things will be made new—better than Eden. This is where God's story lands—with a new beginning, a fresh start.

In the middle of our trials, we remember another story. A story of creation, fall, redemption, and consummation. A story in which Eve and Mary were key players, but in which Jesus was the hero. This other story offers us true comfort: we are greatly loved, so much so that God gave his Son to die for us; our sins are forgiven and our debt is paid; and instead of judgment, we anticipate full healing, lasting joy, and eternal, heavenly communion with our Lord. And this other story provides a bigger backdrop for our individual challenges that puts them in perspective and offers us real hope, even when we grasp at it through tears. This hope is more than wishful thinking because it's anchored in the gospel of Jesus Christ and grounded in God's past, present, and future faithfulness to his promises.

Let's keep preaching the truths of the gospel to ourselves: Jesus died for our sins. Redemption has started, and it's spreading. Death doesn't have the final say. There's more to these stories—God's, yours, and mine.

Prayer

Dear Lord, our trials can weigh so heavily on us. When they do, remind us that our greatest problem isn't how motherhood hasn't gone according to our plans; our greatest problem is our sin, and you already dealt with that on the cross. Our sins are forgiven, and our future hope is secure. Let this reality permeate our thoughts and fill us with deep comfort even in our hardest parenting moments. And you, who graciously gave your Son, how will you not also give us all things (Rom. 8:32)? We boldly ask you to work for our good and your glory in our families. In Jesus's name, amen.

Bible Verses

Gen. 1:1–3:24	John 2:1–12; 9:3; 16:33;
1 Sam. 2:1–10	19:25
Matt. 1:21	Rom. 3:23; 6:23;
Mark 2:5	8:20–23; 10:9
Luke 1:26–38, 46–55;	1 Cor. 13:12; 15:3
2:19, 35, 45	Rev. 19:11; 21:3–5

Reflection Questions

1. How does the "other story" of the Bible help you make sense of the painful parts of your own story?

2. Besides your sin, what *feels* like the biggest problem in your life right now? How do the truths of the gospel speak to that problem?

3. What difference does it make in your trial, knowing that Jesus not only suffered but that he suffered for *you*?

4. What are some of the things we can look forward to in heaven?

5. What part of the gospel do you need to preach to yourself today?

5

So Many Questions

WHEN OUR PASTOR AND HIS WIFE, Warren and Kim, came to visit us in the hospital after our first son was born, they oohed and aahed over our sweet boy and congratulated Scott and me. Despite the feeding challenges and exhaustion, I remember an overall feeling of wonder at new motherhood—the wonder of caressing and nurturing a helpless baby, and the wonder that we were responsible for his care. Awed by all that was set before us in the package of this swaddled infant, I asked Warren for whatever wisdom he might offer us. Behind my one question, a host of others lined up: What do I do if . . . ? What do I do when . . . ? How do I parent our son so that . . . ?

That day in the mother-baby unit of the hospital, I wanted a roadmap to set me on a straight course for the rest of motherhood. Over the years, those early questions have been followed by so many more, and the trials of motherhood have only added more questions to their number: How will their genetic condition play out in my children's lives? How should I pray for them—for healing, for protection? What activities are no longer safe for them, and how do I explain that to them? What does this diagnosis mean for their future?

Similarly, when my mom learned about my missing and misshapen vertebrae when I was an infant, she had her own list of questions about the future: Would her daughter (me) ever walk, or would she be confined to a wheelchair? Since surgery was assumed, how long could it be postponed? Would her little girl ever be able to have children of her own?

You probably have questions of your own, or you're trying to help someone who does. Yours could be wisdom-related. They could concern the past, present, or future. Or they could have to do with God's ways and purposes. Do any of the following questions sound familiar?

Why is God allowing this trial in our lives?

Is this my fault?

Where did I go wrong?

Am I being punished—or is my child being punished—for my sins?

How could God really love us if he allows this—whatever *this* is—in our lives?

When, if ever, will our lives get easier?

What does the future hold for our family—will my child even grow up?

Many biblical figures asked God questions, and to do so isn't necessarily sinful—it's a matter of the heart. Do our questions rise from a rebellious heart or a submissive one? Having already judged

God, do we now toss our scornful accusations at him in the form of questions? Or do our questions overflow from broken, contrite spirits? Genuinely desiring wisdom from our heavenly Father, do we seek his guidance and help for our perplexities? Just as biblical lament invites us to bring our grief to the Lord, in humility, we can bring our honest questions to our heavenly Father.

When we open our Bibles, we read many of the Lord's answers to our queries. For example, consider the question about suffering and punishment. As mentioned in the previous chapter, life in a fallen world explains much of our pain. God's word tells us that sometimes there *is* a connection between our sins, or the sins of others, and the suffering we experience; that was certainly true for the nation of Israel in the Old Testament. Not only does sin lead to natural consequences, but like any loving, human father, God disciplines his children for their good, "that we may share his holiness" (Heb. 12:10). But while suffering can be God's disciplinary tool, it's important to remember that in his hands it always serves a good purpose.

When we run to Jesus, repent of our sins, and trust him for salvation, a holy exchange takes place. We are no longer held *culpable* for our sins; instead, when Jesus died on the cross, he took all the punishment that our past, present, and future sins deserved (Heb. 10:10–14). So when we suffer as moms, it's not because God still has to punish us just a little bit more. No, that would be saying that Jesus's sacrifice wasn't enough, which would be horribly untrue. Our suffering may have a disciplinary purpose (which also suggests a sanctifying purpose), but our heavenly Father's discipline doesn't reflect any change in—but rather affirms—our status as his daughters. Chapter 7 will examine some of the Lord's good purposes in our suffering, and in chapter 8 we'll address more of the lies we can be tempted to believe as moms.

But while the Bible does answer many of our questions, it also leaves room for mystery. It tells us to love God and one another today, and it tells us what we can look forward to in heaven someday, but it doesn't tell us what tomorrow's temperature will be, let alone what good or bad news we'll receive. It offers a story that helps make sense of yours and mine, but it doesn't spell out all the particulars that we can be so eager to know—the details of when and what and how and where and why. Instead, it tells us *who* and what we can expect of him, and it invites us to bring our perplexities to him when they trouble us. God's word reminds us that all of the Christian life—including motherhood—is meant to be lived by faith in the Lord.

The Bible Tells Us Who

Even though there's a particular suffering we face as moms, we aren't the only ones who experience pain related to parenting. The Bible includes fathers who suffered deep loss and grief related to their children. King David prayed and fasted during his infant son's illness, not stopping until his boy had died. Then he said, "I shall go to him, but he will not return to me" (2 Sam. 12:23), a resigned goodbye to a child he wouldn't know on this side of heaven. There's the man who brought his demon-possessed son to Jesus, saying, "But if you can do anything, have compassion on us and help us" (Mark 9:22). When Jesus challenged this father's faith, the poor man said to Jesus, "'I believe; help my unbelief!'" And Jesus commanded the unclean spirit to come out of his son (9:24–25). Then there's Job. In addition to losing his property and health, his seven sons and three daughters died in a single day. Job's story was one the Lord used to encourage me as I processed my miscarriage and the underlying thoughts and emotions it provoked, and it offers one of the strongest examples of God answering a parent's *why* questions with *who*.

Sadly, instead of helping her husband face these calamities with faith in God, Job's wife told him to "curse God and die" (Job 2:9). Overwhelmed by her losses, her grief was understandable; it doesn't take too much imagination to see how, apart from God's grace, sorrow might lead you or me to a similar place. But contrasted with her husband's, her words highlight how remarkable Job's response—and in fact his characteristic mindset throughout the book—was. He said, "'Shall we receive good from God, and shall we not receive evil?' In all this Job did not sin with his lips" (2:10). These two perspectives, Job's and his wife's, beg us to ask ourselves, How do we tend to respond to our motherhood trials? Like Job's wife, it's normal to feel shocked, despairing, angry, worried, or defeated. I've felt all of the above. But these don't have to be our default responses. Instead, with God's help, faith can still be our resting place, and storms and tears and pain don't change that.

To be clear, a faith response doesn't equal going about our business as usual, pretending as if nothing hard is going on. Job breaks that stereotype. Completely humbled, Job sat in the dust and scratched his scabby flesh with a piece of broken pottery. He didn't stuff his emotions; his suffering led him to biblical lament, and his lament included asking God hard questions. To get a sense of Job's honesty, here are a few verses from chapter 3:

> Why is light given to him who is in misery,
>   and life to the bitter in soul,

who long for death, but it comes not,
>and dig for it more than for hidden treasures,
who rejoice exceedingly
>and are glad when they find the grave? (3:20–22)

Job wasn't afraid to ask God why he was still alive, why God didn't just take him. In Job 7, this godly man asked God *what* and *how* and, once again, *why*:

What is man, that you make so much of him,
>and that you set your heart on him,
visit him every morning
>and test him every moment?
How long will you not look away from me,
>nor leave me alone till I swallow my spit?

If I sin, what do I do to you, you watcher of mankind?
>Why have you made me your mark?
>Why have I become a burden to you? (7:17–20)

Job's questions didn't beat around any bushes; they weren't meant to sound polished. He spoke raw words out of the bitterness of his spirit, and he felt complete freedom to address his perplexities to God. In fact, he didn't want his friends' answers; he demanded that Almighty God speak for himself.

God answered Job with comforting words, but not the kind you or I might expect. His comforting words were more questions—questions that redirected Job to consider that the Almighty is unlike anyone else:

"Where were you when I laid the foundation of the earth" (38:4)? Of course Job wasn't there, but God was.

"Who shut in the sea with doors when it burst out from the womb" (38:8)? The answer is obvious—God did.

"Have you commanded the morning since your days began, and caused the dawn to know its place" (38:12)? Of course Job hadn't.

These were only the beginning of God's questions. He was just getting started.

Like we so often do, Job thought he wanted answers; instead, God's questions reminded Job that what he really needed was to have his gaze lifted to the greatness, power, and holiness of his sovereign God. Job needed to know *who*, which meant that Job needed to know God better.

What We Can Expect When We Don't Know What Else to Expect

Life might not have gone the way Job had expected, but just as God did for Hannah and Mary in their stories, the Lord revealed more of himself to Job in his. At the end of the book, Job said,

> I know that you can do all things,
>   and that no purpose of yours can be thwarted. . . .
> I have uttered what I did not understand,
>   things too wonderful for me, which I did not know. . . .
> I had heard of you by the hearing of the ear,
>   but now my eye sees you;
> therefore I despise myself,
>   and repent in dust and ashes. (42:1–6)

This was the true comfort Job craved: the comfort of repentance and humility that comes with knowing *who* was in charge and *whom* he could trust. He didn't really need explanations for his troubles or an escape from them. Instead, Job longed for assurance that he wasn't alone and that the Almighty heard his cries and understood what was going on—even if Job didn't. And isn't this what our hearts so often desire when life is hard—the comfort of knowing that someone is in charge, that we can trust that someone, and that he cares about us? When we read the New Testament, we find that ultimately, *Jesus* is the answer to all of those questions. And while there's no indication that Job ever understood the full story going on behind the scenes of his sorrow (and it's a fascinating one), Job got to know God better in his trials. And while we may never fully grasp the intricacies of our parenting challenges, we too can get to know our Lord better through them.

We're welcome to bring our questions to the Lord, but that doesn't guarantee desired outcomes. We may or may not get answers in the forms we expect. And they may not be the answers we want, especially if we want something for a wrong reason (James 4:3). But what we *can* expect, when we don't know what else to expect, is that we will better understand God's true character. In a wonderful way, we will find that he isn't like us. He doesn't lie or change his mind (Num. 23:19). And his ways are higher than ours. Though we are slow to forgive, "he will abundantly pardon" (Isa. 55:7). His patience functions differently than ours (2 Pet. 3:15), and his heart toward us is gentle (Matt. 11:29). What's more,

The LORD is righteous in all his ways
   and kind in all his works.

The LORD is near to all who call on him,
   to all who call on him in truth.
He fulfills the desire of those who fear him;
   he also hears their cry and saves them. (Ps. 145:17–19)

Not only can we expect God to reveal more of his true character to us, but we can also expect him to keep his promises to us in Jesus—as we'll consider more in the next chapter.

We Can Bring Our Perplexities to the Lord

We can ask the Lord our questions, but we can also bring him our perplexities. What's the difference? It's one thing to query the Lord for details about how, what, when, where, and why. It's another thing to bring our perplexing circumstances—along with the uncertainties and concerns surrounding them, and the anxiety and care they provoke in our hearts—and lay everything down at Jesus's feet. This is an invitation to cast our cares on the Lord because he cares for us (1 Pet. 5:7). It's one way we "take every thought captive to obey Christ" (2 Cor. 10:5). It's what Paul told the Philippian church to do when he wrote the following: "Do not be anxious about anything"—but instead—"in everything by prayer and supplication with thanksgiving let your requests be made known to God" (Phil. 4:6).

It's not always easy, but it's simpler to bring our perplexities to the Lord than you or I might think. For example, as I lie in bed at night, unable to fall asleep because I keep thinking about how early I have to wake up in the morning to make sure all my children are fed and dressed in order to get to their specialist appointments on time, I take my anxious thoughts captive by praying over my day. When I see the email in my inbox that says my child's new tests results are available for me to view, instead of fretting, I can confess my concern to the Lord and ask for his grace to help me trust him—whatever I might discover.

When we move toward God in our trials, we can expect to get to know him better. As we get to know him better, we learn to trust him more. As we trust him more, we bring our perplexities to him more willingly. As we do, we experience more of his peace: "And the peace of God, which surpasses all understanding, will guard your hearts and your minds in Christ Jesus" (Phil. 4:7). Apart from our troubles, we might never flee to Christ and get to experience the sweetness of his comfort and peace. So we can give thanks even for the trials because they allow us to know him better.

But there's more. When we follow this pattern, we also obey Jesus, who told his disciples not to be anxious. He didn't want them to worry but rather exhorted them: "Seek first the kingdom of God and his righteousness, and all these things will be added to you. Therefore do not be anxious about tomorrow, for tomorrow will be anxious for itself. Sufficient for the day is its own trouble" (Matt. 6:33–34). His message to us in our motherhood challenges is the same. Instead of wringing our hands about our children's future, the Lord wants us to depend on him right where we live—today. We do this by faith, often one baby step at a time.

Motherhood Is by Faith

Going back to the story I began this chapter with, when I asked my pastor for his parenting wisdom so many years ago, Warren's answer was just two words: *by faith*. He was right, and this is the truth that has supported me through my most mundane and profound parenting moments. For a Christian mom, all of life—including motherhood—is by faith (2 Cor. 5:7).

According to its biblical definition, "faith is the assurance of things hoped for, the conviction of things not seen" (Heb. 11:1). Faith assumes a kind of blindness. And isn't that what we moms so often experience on these rockier paths? We can't see clearly. We don't know how long our trials will last or what's waiting for us up ahead. We don't know why God allows certain kinds of suffering or what his purposes are. And while God's word provides several important principles for us to apply in our parenting, such as loving our children (Titus 2:4), it doesn't always prescribe how we're supposed to live them out; instead, it's intentionally broad.

From the blowout diaper that slows us down when we're trying to get out the door to the child who decides to throw a tantrum in the library, from nursing a sick toddler to consoling a depressed teenager, and from an unexpected pregnancy to an unexpected pregnancy loss, how does the Lord invite us to parent? Not by any set formula, not by relying solely on the support of a spouse or parents or babysitters or church youth workers, and not by our own ingenuity. The answer is *by faith*. And this is especially true in trials—when there isn't always an obvious right or wrong way to parent, or a right or wrong decision to make.

How does faith function? When the gospel first arrests our hearts, God's grace works a marvelous change in us. But its transforming effects are meant to continue on, spreading into all areas of our lives. This means that instead of living in our own strength and by our own resources, God's Spirit nudges us to press into our heavenly Father's power and sufficiency (2 Cor. 12:9). In faith, we learn to bring whatever he's given us—or even our lack—and see God do "far more abundantly than all we ask or think" (Eph. 3:20), multiplying the fruit of his Holy Spirit in us and our fruitfulness for his kingdom. This extends to motherhood, where we bring our lack of wisdom and ask God for his. We bring our lack of patience in exchange for his. We bring our doubts and fears and ask for his courage. And we bring our questions and, by faith, ask for more faith.

Thankfully, God is more than able to handle a struggling mom's questions—even when that struggling mom is you or me. This is a great comfort. Whether or not he answers our questions when or how we expect, we can expect to get to know him better, which is what we really need. And when our perplexities trouble us, we can bring them all to him with the hope of receiving his peace in exchange. Along the way, we learn that Christian motherhood was never meant to be by sight; it's always been by faith.

Prayer

Dear Lord, thank you for inviting us to bring our questions and perplexities directly to you. As we do, help us get to know you better and trust you more. Teach us what it means to mother by faith, especially through the trials of motherhood. In Jesus's name, amen.

Bible Verses

Num. 23:19

2 Sam. 12:23

Job 2:9–10; 3:20–22;
   7:17–20; 38:4, 8, 12;
   42:1–6

Ps. 145:17–19

Isa. 55:7

Matt. 6:33–34; 11:29

Mark 9:22

2 Cor. 5:7; 10:5; 12:9

Eph. 3:20

Phil. 4:6–7

Titus 2:4

Heb. 10:10–14; 11:1

James 4:3

1 Pet. 5:7

2 Pet. 3:15

Reflection Questions

1. If you could ask God any question about a trial you face, what would it be?

2. Considering Job and his wife, how do you tend to respond to your parenting challenges?

3. How does Job's story offer hope and comfort to yours?

4. What would it look like to exercise faith in God in your current situation?

5. Take a few minutes to pray for your family.

6

God Is Still Good

IN TRIALS, IT'S EASY TO QUESTION the Lord's character, promises, or ways—especially when our experiences don't jive with our self-defined expectations of God. For example, it would seem that a genuinely good Father would heal a sick child or protect a preteen from an abuser. But when God doesn't intervene and evil appears to prevail, does that mean that our heavenly Father isn't really good? Or if he's good, he isn't really powerful?

The evil one would like us to think so. Just as he deceived Eve in Eden, the enemy of our souls continues to both whisper and shout accusations into our ears, urging us to give up our faith, and, in the words of Job's wife, "curse God" (Job 2:9). But there's another way, and as we turn our attention to it in the second half of this book, we're going to seek this path together.

A U.S. federal agent doesn't study counterfeit bills to recognize a counterfeit. He or she learns the characteristics of the real thing. And if we're going to discern and combat the lies of our enemy, first we need to fix our gaze on the truths of Scripture. That's why we'll spend this chapter considering God's character and promises as revealed in his word. Then, with an understanding of who God is and what he has said, we'll have a basis for trusting him in his actions, which we'll explore in chapter 7. In chapter 8, we'll use what we've learned about God, his words, and his ways to speak truth to some of the lies that can derail suffering moms. This may sound heady, but it's immensely practical and has helped me so much.

Who God Is, What He Says, and Why It Matters

As we've already observed in the life of Hannah and other biblical figures, when we run to the Lord rather than away from him in our trials, depend on his grace instead of hide from him in our struggles, and pour out our hearts before him as an alternative to numbing ourselves with any number of lesser things, we get to know him better. When we truly seek him, we find him (Matt. 7:7). We learn who he really is—and isn't. We also find that God's character (who he *is*) and his promises (what he *says*) are so closely related that they're almost identical. And both are trustworthy.

To start, we should remember that "all Scripture is breathed out by God and profitable for teaching" (2 Tim. 3:16). *All Scripture*—not just passages about women and children and motherhood—is immensely helpful to us as we travel our hard motherhood roads. We might know this in our heads, but isn't it tempting to wonder how Scripture connects to the nitty-gritty of our Tuesday afternoons, when the kids are cranky and a husband is running late at work? Without even realizing we do it, it's easy to compartmentalize our personal Bible study or Sunday's sermon from our motherhood trials, to treat them as functionally separate from a child's learning challenges or insulin shots. In this chapter, as we reflect on God's character as it relates to his promises, we'll relate what we learn to the spaces where you and I actually spend our allotted minutes and hours.

All God is and all he says is always relevant to all of us. His character matters when you or I try to console a crying daughter, whether she spills tears because her homework feels too hard or the boy she likes doesn't know her name. Our Lord's promises strengthen us for daily caregiving, and they are our true lifelines when we have to call 911 or race an unconscious child to the hospital.

In both the mundane and heart-pounding moments of motherhood, knowing that God's character and promises aren't distant theological abstractions but truths about the God who is *with us* makes all the difference. And while we could pick any number of Scripture passages to consider who God is and what he says to us, we're going to focus our attention on who God reveals himself to be in Exodus and what he promises there. Along the way, we'll tie these truths to Jesus and see how they meet us where we live.

God Hears and Sees, and He Keeps His Promises

We might think of God's character and promises as two separate things, but it's better to think of them together. That's because what God says flows from who he is; he only speaks what is consistent with his character, and what he speaks carries the full weight and authority of his being. We see this particularly in the book of Exodus where God's promise-keeping nature is on vivid display. He is the God of Abraham, Isaac, and Jacob, who promised in Genesis to make this family into a great nation and give them a new home in a promised land. But famine struck, and Jacob (also called Israel) and his family moved to Egypt where there was food. In Egypt, God kept his promise to multiply their numbers, but over time they were forced to "work as slaves" (Ex. 1:13). When they cried for rescue, "God remembered his covenant. . . . God saw the people of Israel—and God knew" (2:24–25).

God heard his people's cries, remembered his promises, and intended to keep his word. He saw his people, knew what was going on, and planned to do something about their suffering. He determined to "come down to deliver them" (3:8)—a pattern of God's throughout Scripture.

The people of Israel may have felt forsaken or forgotten, just as we can in our trials, but they weren't. God heard every prayer. He saw every form of mistreatment they suffered. He knew the burdens, fears, and anxieties they carried along with each brick for their taskmasters, and he cared enough to extend himself on behalf of his people. He met them more than halfway—he came down to them.

Moms, God hears every prayer you pray for your children. He sees what you and they are walking through. He knows all of it, including all the messy and unmentionable parts. And he sent Jesus to meet you more than halfway—to come down to you. Jesus is Immanuel, "which means, God with us" (Matt. 1:23), the fulfillment of God's promise spoken through Isaiah (Isa. 7:14). Jesus is the one who came to earth, suffered for your sin, and rose again. He is your proof of God's care for you, and he is the one who walks with you on your difficult motherhood path. Jesus knows the heavy load you carry, and he invites you to exchange it for his: "Come to me, all who labor and are heavy laden, and I will give you rest. Take my yoke upon you, and learn from me, for I am gentle and lowly in heart, and you will find rest for your souls. For my yoke is easy, and my burden is light" (Matt. 11:28–30).

God isn't distant or far off, but "gentle and lowly," and he came to dwell with you. He hears, sees, and knows you, your family, and your situation. Just as he kept his promise to deliver Israel from Egypt and to give his Son, Jesus, to deliver you from your sin, he will keep all his promises to you in your hardship—whether in this life or the next—because he is a promise-keeping God.

The Lord Is the Great "I Am"

God came down to Israel because it was time for him to show his true character and keep his promises. It was time for deliverance *from* Egypt and *for* joy, celebration, and worship. It was time for God's people to begin their journey home. One of the first things he did was to reveal himself to an unlikely man named Moses, Pharaoh's adopted grandson and a runaway-turned-shepherd. And Moses posed a question: What if they—the people of Israel—wanted to know God's name (Ex. 3:13)? How should he answer? "God said to Moses, 'I am who I am. . . . Say this to the people of Israel, "The Lord, the God of your fathers, the God of Abraham, the God of Isaac, and the God of Jacob, has sent me to you." This is my name forever, and thus I am to be remembered'" (3:14–15).

God made it clear that his name (what he is *called*) and character (who he *is*) are intertwined: his name is who he is. And what did he call himself? "I am who I am." First, such a name draws attention to his attributes as self-existent, unchanging, and the Creator and sustainer of all that exists.[1] Embedded in these verses is also a reminder of the history that the Lord and Israel shared. Next, this name would outlast that generation. It's who God would be for all eternity. Finally, this un-dependent, always-the-same, and original-designer was the same God who promised Moses, "But I will be with you" (Ex. 3:12). Knowing God's name and character, Moses could trust his promises. Moses and the Israelites didn't have to fear, no matter how difficult it would be to leave Egypt or how challenging the journey to the promised land would turn out to be, because the God who created and sustained them was the Lord who would travel with them.

It's no wonder, then, that the Pharisees wanted to throw stones at Jesus when he said, "Before Abraham was, I am" (John 8:58). These religious leaders knew that when Jesus referred to himself as "I am," he identified himself with a holy God, one who was entirely unlike them, one who existed before anything they could see or touch, one whose name was so great that in Hebrew it was only written with consonants and no vowels, out of respect for and to protect its purity.[2] Jesus's claim would have been blasphemous if it hadn't been so gloriously true, but he really is "the image of the invisible God, the firstborn of all creation. For by him all things were created . . .

---

1 Kenneth Laing Harris, study notes for Exodus 3:14–15 in *ESV Study Bible* (Wheaton, IL: Crossway, 2008), 149.

2 Jesus made seven "I am" statements in the book of John: *I am the bread of life* (6:35, 48, 51); *I am the light of the world* (8:12; 9:5); *I am the door of the sheep* (10:7, 9); *I am the good shepherd* (10:11, 14); *I am the resurrection and the life* (11:25); *I am the way, the truth, and the life* (14:6); and *I am the true vine* (15:1). I am grateful to the editors of the *ESV Study Bible* for compiling this information in chart form (Wheaton, IL: Crossway, 2008), 2041.

through him and for him. . . . For in him all the fullness of God was pleased to dwell, and through him to reconcile to himself all things . . . making peace by the blood of his cross" (Col. 1:15–20).

Jesus didn't merely *profess* to be God, but he *was* and *is* and *will* be Lord over all. He is united with our promise-keeping God: "In him all the fullness of God was pleased to dwell." And he is the fulfillment of his promises: "making peace by the blood of his cross." Jesus is both.

So, a question: How well do you remember your history with Jesus? Do you remember how you were dead, and he made you alive? What struggles has he already so lovingly carried you through? Like Israel throughout the Old Testament, we can be so quick to forget our Lord's past faithfulness. But "Jesus Christ is the same yesterday and today and forever" (Heb. 13:8). He doesn't grow fickle in his affections toward you and me. He remains the same Jesus whose light shone in the darkness of our hearts when we were first saved, and his promise to his followers is still true for us: "I am with you always, to the end of the age" (Matt. 28:20). Jesus didn't come to be with his people for only a short lifespan over two thousand years ago; through the gift of the Holy Spirit, he lives in us and we live in him today.

When God appeared to Moses, proclaimed his name, and told him that he would be with Israel, he didn't say the exodus would be easy. Or that the people would always believe and never doubt God's power. Or that the way would always be clear or that there wouldn't be any enemies lying in wait, ready to pounce. And when you and I turned to Jesus for salvation, though we experienced marvelous rescue and deliverance, it didn't mean that our journeys toward heaven would be without toils and snares. What sets us apart as Christian women isn't easier passage but the presence of our glorious Savior with all his attributes. We get Jesus in his entirety—for eternity. We enjoy union with Christ, the one who saved us from our greatest problem of sin, as we travel even the hardest roads.

God Is Gloriously Good

God kept his promise and miraculously delivered his people from Pharaoh's army (Ex. 14–15), but in the same book, we read how quickly the Israelites forgot God's powerful rescue and turned to worship idols. Because of Israel's disobedience, the Lord told Moses that he would "send an angel" before them, but he wouldn't go up with them himself (33:2–3). But this option was totally unacceptable to Moses, who remembered God's initial promise and knew that the Lord's presence was the only thing that distinguished God's people from the surrounding nations. Moses pleaded with God not only to go with them, but to show his glory—and, remarkably, God agreed. "He said, 'I will make all my goodness pass before you and will proclaim before you my name "The LORD"'" (33:19).

We know what it's like for devastating news to send our heads spinning; we get gut-punching disappointment. But Moses was about to fall to the ground for a totally different reason. He would bow his head and worship God for his *glorious goodness*. As he passed before Moses, the Lord proclaimed: "The LORD, the LORD, a God merciful and gracious, slow to anger, and abounding in steadfast love and faithfulness, keeping steadfast love for thousands, forgiving iniquity and transgression and sin" (Ex. 34:6–7).

Here is God's answer to our question, "Is God really good?" Yes, God is good. That's who he declares himself to be. But how good is he? Wrapped up in his glorious goodness is his mercy and grace, enough for today and tomorrow. It includes all the patience and forbearance he demonstrates when he's slow to anger with our stubborn and persistent sin. His constantly flowing, bottomless fountain of love and faithfulness offers us true and lasting security. And his full and complete forgiveness awaits when we return to him after doubting his love, wandering away from his fatherly embrace, or transgressing his commands.

When God's glory moved near Moses, this man of God was hidden in the cleft of a rock. Only after God had passed by was Moses allowed to see him; even then, he saw only God's back. But "God, who said, 'Let light shine out of darkness,' has shone in our hearts to give the light of the knowledge of the glory of God in the face of Christ" (2 Cor. 4:6). In Christ, we comprehend more of God's glory than Moses did. Not only that, but on an already-determined day, we will see our Savior face to face.

God is still good—for us—in our present challenges. Through Jesus, the Lord isn't far off but *with us*, in all his glorious goodness, in our kitchens and carpools and medical appointments. He doesn't go on vacation when our trials come; he's with us when we answer the phone calls that make our bodies shake. He isn't taking a nap or scrolling the internet when a child falls down the stairs, flips a bicycle, or crashes a car. He's right there with us, his hand holding ours (Ps. 139:10), when we wonder whether a child's mental health will improve or worsen. He is with us, and he is good.

Where We Live

In this book's introduction, I wrote about my mom's dawning realization that I didn't remember many of the details surrounding my childhood diagnosis of kyphoscoliosis, as well as a host of other memories that were still so fresh and packed with emotion for her. Although I had lived the experience with her, and it was part of what made me who I am, I listened that day as more of an observer than a participant as she invited me to reenter our shared story.

She led me from the kitchen, upstairs to the second floor, and through two doors to the bedroom I had grown up in. But it hadn't been my bedroom when the scene she described took place. Back then it was an attic, and she showed me where she had stood by her ironing board when she had pleaded with the Lord to lift the dark and heavy cloud that had descended over her, encompassing her first experience of motherhood and robbing her of joy. She craved a "normal" childhood for me, one undisturbed by alarming concerns or interrupted by the fears and anxieties that doctors had forecasted.

She showed me where she had stood, where she had wept. And there—she pointed with her finger to the spot on the floor—God had met her, a suffering mom, on a day that looked just like any other. Like Mary, she hadn't been looking for a story. And similar to Hannah, she had known there wasn't anywhere else for her to go. But in the middle of ironing clothes she cried out to the Lord, and he heard her, right there in southern New Jersey. He met her with the assurance of his presence and peace. He comforted her with truths she needed to hear, assuring her that he heard her cries and she could trust him. And the cloud lifted.

When my children were diagnosed with Alpha-1, the Lord met me in his word. There was little time to write in my journal in that intense season, but I began writing a list of Bible verses about trusting God, adding quotations and encouragements from friends so I could remember his goodness in one of the hardest seasons of my life. As difficult as those days were, the promises of God's word fed and sustained me. (See Appendix A: Go-To Bible Verses.)

Our God hears, sees, and keeps his promises. He is the great "I AM"—our self-existent, unchanging, creating, and sustaining Lord. And he is gloriously good—full of mercy, grace, love, faithfulness, and forgiveness. God's character, including these and many more attributes described in his word, offer great comfort to hurting moms. How can this be? Because we know who God is, we know he is *for us* right in the middle of our real lives. And because God already kept his promises in sending Jesus, through whom all his promises are yes and amen (2 Cor. 1:20), we take him at his word and expect him to keep all his promises to us. With assurance of his character and promises, we're encouraged to trust his ways. As we'll consider next, this includes believing him when he says that "for those who love God all things work together for good" (Rom. 8:28)—even when we can't yet see the good that's being worked.

Prayer

Dear Lord, when we consider your character and promises, what can we do but worship you? You are Lord, and there is none like you. Holy is your name! Thank you for hearing our prayers, seeing our sorrows, and coming down to us. We praise your glorious goodness, revel in your mercy and grace, wonder at your love and faithfulness, and gratefully accept your forgiveness. Especially in our motherhood trials, remind us of who you are and your promises, and teach us to trust you. In Jesus's name, amen.

Bible Verses

Ex. 1:13; 2:24–25; 3:8,
    12–15; 14–15; 33:2–3,
    19; 34:6–7
Job 2:9
Ps. 139:10
Matt. 1:23; 7:7; 11:28–30;
    28:20

John 8:58
Rom. 8:28
2 Cor. 1:20; 4:6
Col. 1:15–20
2 Tim. 3:16
Heb. 13:8

Reflection Questions

1. What's a question you have asked about God's character in a motherhood trial?

2. What makes it hard for you to remember God's character and promises on your Tuesday afternoons—or any other time of the week that isn't set apart for Bible study and prayer?

3. Which of God's promises has become dear to you in your challenge?

4. When has God met you in your everyday, maybe when you least expected him?

5. Take some time to read Exodus 33:12–34:9 and reflect on who God reveals himself to be. Why do you think he focused on the qualities mentioned in 34:6–7 when he could have named others?

7

God Is Doing Something

YOU AND I MIGHT NOT KNOW what God is doing in our pain, but he's doing something. Even if we did know his purposes, we might not understand them. But he's still doing something. Does the sun stop shining when it's hidden behind the clouds? No, it keeps on shining as brightly as ever. We just can't see it. Similarly, if we accept God to *be* who he says he is—gloriously good—then we have every reason to believe that his *ways* are also glorious and good, even when what he's doing is hidden from our view. And that's just what Romans 8 tells us to expect. As we learn to trust God's character and promises, his word becomes increasingly dear to us, and the soaring truths of Romans 8 are especially rich with hope and comfort for moms who suffer.

The apostle Paul opens this marvelous chapter with a breathtaking reminder that "there is therefore now no condemnation for those who are in Christ Jesus" (Rom. 8:1). Our condemnation was done away with at the cross where Jesus died. Instead, we who were once separated from God, are *in* Christ—hidden, sheltered, secure, and inseparable from him. And "if the Spirit of him who raised Jesus from the dead dwells in you, he who raised Christ Jesus from the dead will also give life to your mortal bodies through his Spirit who dwells in you" (8:11). No longer dead in our sin, our new, resurrected lives have already begun. These lives aren't characterized by slavery or fear (8:15) but by adoption as God's children and a shared inheritance with Christ (8:15–17). Yet even real, spiritual life in Christ—for our earthly days—includes trials and suffering.

Motherhood doesn't always deliver what we hope, and it frequently delivers hurts we don't expect. Real life in a fallen world includes heartache and loss, loneliness and hunger, disappointment and broken trust, shattered dreams and sleepless nights. But listen to what Pastor John Piper says of Romans 8:

> What makes this chapter so great is the absolute realism for mothers of the kinds of hardships and losses and difficulties and setbacks and pain they are all going to have to walk through. It's utterly wide-eyed to the sufferings of the world with its roots sitting unshakably deep into the massive things of God. It knows when believing mothers walk through the deepest waters, they are not encountering wrath. . . . These are disciplinary acts of God to fit a mother for heaven and for the most fruitful life on earth.[1]

Yes, God's word is "utterly wide-eyed to the sufferings of the world," yet, at the same time, Romans 8 shows us that our suf-

---

1   The Risen Motherhood Team, "Episode 162: John Piper's Encouragement for Moms in Suffering Transcript" (Risen Motherhood, April 22, 2020). https://www.risen motherhood.com/.

fering isn't pointless but purposeful: God is doing something, as Piper explains, to fit us for heaven and for fruitful lives on earth. Specifically, our *gloriously good* God is preparing a future-oriented *glory* and working for our present-oriented *good* in our suffering.

God Is Preparing a Future-Oriented Glory for Us

We've already encountered the idea of glory in Exodus, where God's glory passed by Moses, but now we note it again in Romans 8, which talks about a breathtaking glory that Christians will receive. Paul wrote, "For I consider that the sufferings of this present time"—including our sorrows connected with motherhood—"are not worth comparing with the glory that is to be revealed to us" (Rom. 8:18). What did Paul mean "not worth comparing"? No matter how dark our path, this glory shines brighter; regardless of how great our losses, this glory is greater; and even if our wounds are tender to the touch, this glory extends full healing and restoration. But though we suffer in a variety of ways in this "present time," this glory is yet to be revealed; it is future-oriented. There's no question that we *will* experience it, but we must *wait* for it. It's for this glory that we "groan inwardly as we wait eagerly for adoption" (8:23).

Though we've been saved and God's Spirit dwells in us, we still groan when our children suffer. We writhe in agony over what diagnoses might mean for their future. We wrestle with the realities of adapting a living space to accommodate a wheelchair or welcoming a new caregiver into our inner circle. We struggle as we navigate an imperfect foster care system. Redemption has started, but we wait for its consummation. But as believing women, we do so with hope (Rom. 8:24). Things might get worse before they get better, but they will get better. We don't lose heart but cling to the promise that our "light momentary affliction is preparing for us an eternal weight of glory beyond all comparison" (2 Cor. 4:17). Though the days be long, our suffering is "light" and "momentary" compared to eternity. And it is preparing glory for us that outweighs our suffering on any scale.

Glory isn't an ethereal thing but something our Lord prepares for us to partake of. As we suffer with Christ, we will "also be glorified with him" (Rom. 8:17). We will one day taste "the freedom of the glory of the children of God" (8:21). And though this is a future-oriented reality, it's as certain as our salvation, for "those whom he predestined he also called, and those whom he called he also justified, and those whom he justified he also glorified" (8:30). Do you notice how God's future-oriented glory for his children is described in the past tense? In God's book, our glory is so sure that it's as good as done.

God Is Working for Our Present-Oriented Good

But as we wait for this future glory, God is working a present-oriented good for us. Even now, his Spirit "helps us in our weakness" (Rom. 8:26). When we don't know what or how to pray for our children, he "intercedes for us with groanings too deep for words" (8:26). When we can't express what we're going through, he who "searches hearts" also knows God's will and asks accordingly—on our behalf (8:27). What's more, the midsection of Romans 8 leads us to this life-giving, assurance-boosting promise: "For those who love God all things work together for good, for those who are called according to his purpose" (8:28).

On a recent road trip I circumvented three detours, but it wasn't until my minivan was totally stopped, bumper to bumper with a stalled semitruck, that I realized I wasn't going anywhere. There had been an accident nearby, and as a result I was sitting in an unexpected parking lot. When a severe hardship or deep tragedy brings life to a standstill, sometimes we find ourselves sitting in our own figurative parking lots. There's nothing we can do to change anything. We just have to wait them out. And in those often heart-racing and nail-biting places, the hope-filled promise of Romans 8:28 is one we want to have memorized—because it tells us that our fear, lack of control, and confusion aren't pointless. God isn't just doing something for some far-off future, but he's doing something right now. In our unexpected "parking lots," he is working for our good—not in spite of the blockage, but in it and through its implications—because *he* is good.

Our greatest good isn't a solution, healing, a vacation, or even a restored relationship with an estranged child—as wonderful as each of these things is. For those who love God and are called by him, the good that our heavenly Father has in mind for us is "to be conformed to the image of his Son" (Rom. 8:29), to be pressed into his mold. It's for us to become more like Jesus, our older brother (8:29). We're to sound more like him and act more like him and bear a greater resemblance to him. Jesus "learned obedience through what he suffered" (Heb. 5:8), so we shouldn't be surprised if the same is true for us. Before we continue further in Romans 8, let's consider some ways that God works "all things"—even our most horrific sufferings—"together for good" to make us more like Jesus (Rom. 8:28).[2]

2   Some of this content first appeared in "8 Ways Trials Help Us," an article I wrote for The Gospel Coalition, November 18, 2020, https://www.thegospelcoalition.org/.

1. Trials Deepen Our Prayer Lives

Throughout the Gospels, prayer was Jesus's habit. We observe this in the first chapter of Mark: "And rising very early in the morning, while it was still dark, [Jesus] departed and went out to a desolate place, and there he prayed" (Mark 1:35). In the Sermon on the Mount, Jesus taught his followers how to pray in accordance with his Father's will. And on the night of his betrayal, when Jesus's "sweat became like great drops of blood falling down to the ground," he demonstrated the full extent of submissive prayer when he pleaded with his Father to "remove this cup from me. Nevertheless, not my will, but yours, be done" (Luke 22:42, 44).

When our trials throw us to our knees in prayer, they are being used to make us look and act more like Jesus. In the throes of worry, we can "let [our] requests be made known to God" and cast all our "anxieties on him, because he cares for [us]" (Phil. 4:6; 1 Pet. 5:7). Such humble prayer bears good fruit in our lives as we too learn to submit to God's will and obey him. It cultivates dependence on God, attacks our pride, and positions us to delight in the Lord who hears and answers in accordance with his wisdom.

2. Trials Increase Our Knowledge of God's Character and Word

After Jesus had fasted for forty days in the wilderness, the devil tempted him to turn stones into bread. How did Jesus answer him? He quoted Deuteronomy 8:3, reminding Satan that "man shall not live by bread alone, but by every word that comes from the mouth of God" (Matt. 4:4). When our motherhood challenges lead us into wilderness seasons, we also do well to remember God's character and promises as revealed in his word (as we discussed in chap. 6).

When so much was unsure following my children's diagnosis with Alpha-1, and when I felt so unsteady after my miscarriage, God's word offered me a stability that other things couldn't. While I was comforted by the presence of my family in those times, motherhood as an entity had certainly proven unreliable. And although my husband and I supported and cared for one another through those difficult days, we needed something stronger than our marriage to fall back on. God's word was the bedrock that kept us from sinking. If you open the Bible to study God's character and internalize his promises on your own dark days, God will use your suffering to grow your knowledge of his character and his word in a way that causes you to resemble Jesus more closely.

3. Trials Equip Us to Comfort Others

In chapter 2, we touched on how, just as he did for Paul, God "comforts us in all our affliction, so that we may be able to comfort those who are in any affliction" (2 Cor. 1:4). This is one of our Lord's beautiful purposes in our pain. But do you remember how this strengthening comfort comes to us? This comfort comes through Jesus. "For as we share abundantly in Christ's sufferings, so *through Christ* we share abundantly in comfort" (1:5).

If we share in Christ's sufferings, we will be comforted through him. But "share abundantly in Christ's sufferings" includes more than being persecuted for our faith, although it includes that and some moms experience it. These sufferings consist of a variety of trials associated with faithfulness to God, which might look like the following:

Are you choosing to keep your baby at personal cost to yourself (of reputation, opportunity, or finances) but in obedience to the Lord?

Are you preserving your autistic daughter's dignity as you continue to change her diapers with compassion, even though you've been doing so for more than ten years?

Are you teaching your children about God's design for male and female although they hear something different at school?

Where you share in Christ's sufferings on your motherhood journey, God's comfort is abundantly available to you. And as you experience his comfort, one of God's good purposes in your trial is that you will follow suit and act like your older brother, Jesus, comforting others with the comfort he made possible.

4. Trials Remind Us That Earth Isn't Our True Home

Jesus preached about another kingdom. Of the beginning of Jesus's ministry, Mark wrote, "Jesus came into Galilee, proclaiming the gospel of God, and saying, 'The time is fulfilled, and the kingdom of God is at hand; repent and believe in the gospel'" (Mark 1:14–15). Jesus didn't come to overthrow Rome, the political authority of the day, but to welcome redeemed sinners like you and me into God's everlasting kingdom, and his teachings point us not to earthly wealth or health but to the treasures of this other kingdom. Another way trials work for good in our lives is that they help us see the limitations of the world we live in and increase our longing for the kingdom of God—our true home.

When trials make us feel out of place, we yearn for our true home. In loneliness, we desire God's presence. Tears stir our hearts for a place with no "mourning, nor crying, nor pain anymore" (Rev. 21:4). Sick bodies wait eagerly for new ones. Death makes us long for resurrection. These trials and more remind us that earth isn't our final resting place and increase our hunger for heaven, the kingdom Jesus preached.

5. Trials Test and Strengthen Our Faith

Long before you or I were born, let alone faced any form of pain related to childbearing, Jesus was "the founder and perfecter of our faith, who for the joy that was set before him endured the cross, despising the shame" (Heb. 12:2). Why did the founder and perfector of our faith endure brutal treatment and public nakedness? Why did he swallow the cup of God's wrath? "For the joy that was set before him."

This is where the Bible brings together two unlikely partners, trials and joy. James expressed it this way: "Count it all joy, my brothers, when you meet trials of various kinds, for you know that the testing of your faith produces steadfastness" (James 1:2–3). And Peter added his twist, "In this you rejoice, though now for a little while, if necessary, you have been grieved by various trials, so that the tested genuineness of your faith—more precious than gold that perishes though it is tested by fire—may be found to result in praise and glory and honor at the revelation of Jesus Christ" (1 Pet. 1:6–7).

Isn't this jaw dropping? God can use even the most bitter trials to prove the genuineness of our faith, filling our hearts with joyful assurance of salvation, and ultimately pointing us to Jesus, our champion, the one who ran this race before us. With his example in front of us and his Spirit in us, we can "lay aside every weight, and sin which clings so closely, and . . . run with endurance the race that is set before us" (Heb. 12:1). We do so with the hope of joining him where he "is seated at the right hand of the throne of God" (Heb. 12:2). Through these five examples, and many more, we see that God uses our trials for our present good.

God Is for Us, and Nothing Can Separate Us from His Love

Although we might not understand specifically what God is doing in our current challenges, we can be confident that he is doing something, and that this "something" is vitally connected to our ultimate joy. But there's more to glean from Romans 8. All the previous verses have set us up for verse 31: "What then shall we say to these things? If God is for us, who can be against us?" Yes, if God is using even our trials to prepare future-oriented glory and to work present-oriented good in our lives, we can be sure that he is *for us*. And in case we still doubt, Paul reminds us again— as we regularly ought to remind ourselves—of God's generosity toward us as it is conveyed in the gospel. "He who did not spare his own Son but gave him up for us all, how will he not also with him graciously give us all things?" (8:32). God will supply what we need to keep going. No opposition from our enemy, and no trial we face, can undo what God has begun in our lives. He *will* complete the good work he has started in us (Phil. 1:6).

Who can bring a charge against you? Satan's accusations can't stick. The only one who could bring a charge against you— God—made you right with himself when you placed faith in Jesus (Rom. 8:33). "Who is to condemn?" With Jesus interceding for you, no one can (8:34). And "who shall separate [you] from the love of Christ" (8:35)? Shall miscarriage, secondary infertility, a child who wanders from the faith, or a child's disability? Nothing has that power!

In the next chapter, we'll apply what we've learned about God's character, promises, and ways as we unravel some of the lies that Satan often uses to derail suffering moms. But before we do, let these final verses from Romans 8 sink deep inside you. Read them a few times if needed—do whatever it takes for them to move from your brain to your heart:

> No, in all these things we are more than conquerors through him who loved us. For I am sure that neither death nor life, nor angels nor rulers, nor things present nor things to come, nor powers, nor height nor depth, nor anything else in all creation, will be able to separate us from the love of God in Christ Jesus our Lord. (Rom. 8:37–39)

If you are *in Christ*, nothing can separate you from his love—not even the most trying challenges or devastating losses of motherhood. Not the lies of the evil one. Nothing in all creation. There's no greater hope or comfort for a suffering mom than this, and it's why we can "rejoice in hope of the glory of God" and "rejoice in our sufferings" (Rom. 5:2–3), confident that God is doing something. And since God is the one doing it, we know it will be glorious and good.

Prayer

Dear Lord, so often we can't see what you're doing, but it comforts us to know that you're doing something. Even through our trials, you are preparing a future-oriented glory and working present-oriented good for us, making us more like Jesus. Don't waste these trials in our lives, but redeem them for your purposes. Thank you for the beautiful promises of Romans 8, including these closing assurances that you are for us and not against us and that nothing can separate us from your love. Help us believe and take your words to heart. In Jesus's name, amen.

Bible Verses

Deut. 8:3

Matt. 4:4

Mark 1:14–15, 35

Luke 22:42, 44

Rom. 5:2–3; 8:1–39

2 Cor. 1:4–5; 4:17

Phil. 1:6; 4:6

Heb. 5:8; 12:1–2

James 1:2–3

1 Pet. 1:6–7; 5:7

Rev. 21:4

Reflection Questions

1. What comfort do you find in knowing that God is doing something in your trials, that they aren't pointless but purposeful?

2. What does it mean that God is "preparing for us an eternal weight of glory beyond all comparison" (2 Cor. 4:17), and how does this stir your hope?

3. Of the five listed examples of how God uses trials for our good mentioned in this chapter, which ones resonate with your experience? Is there one that particularly encourages you in your current circumstances?

4. In your challenges, historically or at present, how does it shift your perspective to consider them as opportunities to share in Christ's sufferings?

5. Reread Romans 8 through the lens of your motherhood trial, substituting your name and your hardship where appropriate.

Bonus: memorize Romans 8:28–29.

8

Learning to Talk

SCOTT AND I HAD BEEN MARRIED just over a year, and our first son was only two months old, when my husband left a well-salaried job to study as a full-time student at a pastor's college. We cheerfully closed the door of our first apartment and rented rooms in another family's home several states away, close to the school. However, despite our high hopes for this new and exciting season of our young family's life and the encouraging support of our church, family, and friends, it didn't take long for me to wonder how we were going to pay our bills. When Christmas came, we had less than a hundred dollars in our shared bank account, and I fretted over our finances and future. School costs were covered, but how would we pay for our son's diapers or formula, let alone the rent?

Aware of my anxiety, Warren (my pastor) asked, "What is the worst thing that you think could happen?" It didn't take long to answer. I envisioned myself sitting with my infant son in my lap on a dirty, city sidewalk. In that depressing picture, we were homeless, penniless, and hungry. As I voiced this to Warren, he empathized, but he also reminded me how the Lord had led my husband and me and provided for our family up to that point. Did I really think God would desert us now? And did I really believe, given the support of our Christian community, that there wouldn't be a home for us?

Put that way, my frightened words sounded silly. But before then, I'd never learned to follow my fears to their source. This line of reasoning was unfamiliar to me, and that year the Lord used godly friends to teach me how to discern some of the lies that were entangling me—and then speak truth to them. As I studied God's word, I began to see that fretting about finances, parenting, or anything else was only a surface manifestation of a heart-level problem. My worry and anxiety indicated that no matter what I professed, in my core I wasn't fully trusting God. And even though I would have said that the Lord was my provider, my distress showed that I doubted his ability—or was it his willingness?—to provide. Mingled with those doubts was another question: Did God really care about us? It was time for some biblical heavy lifting.

When I got a few hours to myself on a Saturday, I created a chart. In one column was a list of my worries. Then I began translating those worries into what they revealed I actually believed about God—not what I would have told someone I believed about God, but what my anxieties demonstrated I *functionally* believed about God. Once I did that, it was easier to discern the lies at play. For each untruth, I searched the Bible for a verse about God's character or one of his promises to combat it. This practice has continued to serve me well.

At the beginning of chapter 6, I explained that we need to study what the Bible reveals about God's character, promises, and ways if we're going to be able to distinguish between what is true and what isn't. While I recommend that we do this important work in the quieter seasons of life to equip us for the more intense ones, it's in our trials that this labor is put to the test. Does what we believe hold up when it's put through the fire? And though I know firsthand how hard it can be to prioritize reading Scripture or the preaching of God's word after several nights spent caring for a newborn, tending to a sick child, or counseling a struggling teen, I'm also convinced that our spiritual lives will be dry if we don't find ways to drink regularly—even small sips in our more challenging times—from the Spirit's well of life-giving water. Whether you're in the middle of a storm or experiencing a brief lull, in this chapter we'll take what we've already covered in this book and—just as I learned to do as a new wife and mom—directly apply it to the lies our enemy sends our direction.

Temptation's Tug

But before we dive in, let's briefly talk about suffering and temptation. We shouldn't be surprised when we suffer as moms. As Peter wrote, "Beloved, do not be surprised at the fiery trial when it comes upon you to test you, as though something strange were happening to you" (1 Pet. 4:12). However, even when we have a robust theology of suffering, we can be caught off guard by the temptations to sin that often travel with our trials. They can shake us, causing us to wonder whether our biblical framework is strong enough to stand. A temptation to doubt God can make us feel distant from him. Just think about your own difficulties for a minute. Did a temptation to envy travel with any of them? What about complaining or discontentment, anger or self-pity? Did you ever turn to anything else for comfort—binge-watching, binge-eating, or binge-scrolling—before you turned to Jesus?

If you're anything like me, not only have you felt temptation's tug, but you *have* sinned and *do* sin when life turns sour. But trials aren't an excuse to sin. We read that, despite his extreme losses, "Job did not sin or charge God with wrong" (Job 1:22). Sin is natural, but it isn't inevitable because Jesus broke sin's mastery over us on the cross. There's a way to suffer without sinning, and Jesus is ready to help us. Here's how the author of Hebrews framed it: "For because [Jesus] himself has suffered when tempted, he is able to help those who are being tempted" (Heb. 2:18). Even though he never sinned, Jesus understands temptation. He knows it can bring its own added suffering, and he is both able and willing to help us when it rears its ugly head.

As long as we're breathing, it isn't too late for the gospel to change us. We can repent, ask Jesus to forgive us, and learn to trust him in our trials. When we fall again—which we will, since our fight against sin and the flesh and the devil will remain as long as we're on earth—we ask for Jesus's help—again and again and again. And though we feel like we're taking two steps backward for every step forward, we remember that God is doing something in us along the way—making us more like Jesus—and none of our suffering is wasted in God's economy. Whether we feel like it or not, we *are* making progress as we move toward our heavenly home, and this chapter is another tool to help you on your way.

Talking to Ourselves

If we're going to experience God's hope when motherhood doesn't deliver, and not succumb to temptation and sin, we need to be on guard, recognize our enemy's lies, and fight them with biblical truth. How do we do this? We must learn to talk to ourselves. D. Martyn Lloyd-Jones, a pastor from the twentieth century, wisely instructs us:

> I say that we must talk to ourselves instead of allowing "ourselves" to talk to us! . . . Have you realized that most of your unhappiness in life is due to the fact that you are listening to yourself instead of talking to yourself? Take those thoughts that come to you the moment you wake up in the morning. You have not originated them, but they start talking to you, they bring back the problems of yesterday, etc. Somebody is talking. Who is talking to you? Your self is talking to you. Now [David's] treatment [in Psalm 42] was this: instead of allowing his self to talk to him, he starts talking to himself. "Why art thou cast down, O my soul?" he asks. His soul had been depressing him, crushing him. So he stands up and says: "Self, listen for a moment, I will speak to you."[1]

Lloyd-Jones refers to Psalm 42:5–6, where David took himself to task saying, "Hope in God; for I shall again praise him, my salvation and my God." And when we find ourselves passively absorbing whatever our "selves" throw at us, we too need to take

---

1   D. Martyn Lloyd-Jones, *Spiritual Depression: Its Causes and Its Cure* (repr. 2002; Grand Rapids, MI: Eerdmans, 1965), 20–21.

ourselves in hand and break the looping lies that play in our heads by speaking God's truth to them.

When the devil tempted our Lord in the wilderness, Jesus spoke Scripture back to him. If we're going to counter the deceiver's lies, then we too need to pick up "the sword of the Spirit, which is the word of God" (Eph. 6:17). "For the word of God is living and active, sharper than any two-edged sword, piercing to the division of soul and of spirit, of joints and of marrow, and discerning the thoughts and intentions of the heart" (Heb. 4:12).

Let's try a thought experiment that will help us to do this—since, unless we slow down, many of us are moving so fast that it's easy to miss what's going on inside of us.

1. First, in your head or out loud, name one of your current trials related to motherhood. Then take a minute to listen to yourself. What are some of the first words or thoughts that come to mind about your trial? Maybe you've never put them into words; they're more of a feeling. That's OK. For now, don't try to categorize them as right or wrong, but try instead to listen honestly to what's filling the space between your ears. Pay particular attention to any repeated phrases or thoughts that just keep cycling. Has anything been hanging out in that space for more than an hour, a day, or a week? Write down whatever thoughts or feelings emerge. You don't have to use complete sentences, and no one will check your spelling or grammar. The point here is to pause; instead of mindless listening, pay attention to what you're hearing.

2. Reflect on these feelings and thoughts a little more closely. What do they reveal about what matters to you, or what you're concerned about? Which are the loudest voices, and why do you think that's the case—was there a recent phone call or appointment that brought something to your attention? Should these voices receive as much radio time as they do? Or, to put it another way, do they line up with your priorities? Are there other thoughts embedded in the ones you've already written down—thoughts that beg further exploration?

3. *Now line up what you've written down with God's word.* How do these thoughts and feelings compare with what Scripture reveals about God's character, promises, and ways? Do they involve temporal things, or are they kingdom-minded (Matt. 6:25–33)? How do they hold up when tested with Philippians 4:8: "Finally, brothers, whatever is true, whatever is honorable, whatever is just, whatever is pure, whatever is lovely, whatever is commendable, if there is any excellence, if there is anything worthy of praise, think about these things"? Do they ring true or false?

4. *Confession—not condemnation—comes next.* If you've been honest, at least a few lies have probably emerged. Don't let them lead you down a path of condemnation. Remember Romans 8: "There is therefore now no condemnation for those who are in Christ Jesus. For the law of the Spirit of life has set you free in Christ Jesus" (8:1–2). Resist the lie of condemnation; instead, bring all lies to Jesus. He is able and willing to help you fight them. He's already helped you bring them out of the dark and into the light. If there's any sin to confess, confess it, confident that Jesus will be "faithful and just to forgive us our sins and to cleanse us from all unrighteousness. If we say we have not sinned, we make him a liar, and his word is not in us" (1 John 1:9–10).

5. *Where truth emerges, praise the Lord, but for each lie you've uncovered, prayerfully ask the Lord to lead you to truths that combat it.* Maybe this requires a phone call to a friend, turning to the

concordance at the back of your study Bible, or searching a reliable website. For example, if a recent trip to the grocery store has you concerned about how inflationary prices might squeeze your family's already-tight food budget, and the new price of milk keeps popping up in your head when your growing son pours himself another glass, you might search for references to God as provider. Most likely you'll find a plethora of verses to get you started.

6. *The last step is to choose some of those verses, copy them, and put them where you will see them.* When a lie starts speaking to you, you start talking to it instead. You tell that lie, "No, that's not true! My God is my provider. He owns the cattle on a thousand hills, and he has said that I don't need to worry about what our family will eat. I just need to seek him. So be quiet! Instead of listening to you one more time, *self,* I'm going to talk to Jesus about this."

Common Lies and Truth to Combat Them

Was that experiment helpful? I hope so. But if it was confusing, felt like too much effort, or sounded emotionally difficult to attempt in your current season, I've also compiled a list of ten lies (there are many more) that are common to suffering women. Many of these have already been addressed in this book. For each lie, there's a truth from God's word backed with Scripture. (You can also find them in chart form in appendix B.) I encourage you to read through them prayerfully and see if any resonate with you.

Lie 1: The trial is my enemy.
Truth: Satan is my enemy.

Scripture: "Be sober-minded; be watchful. Your adversary the devil prowls around like a roaring lion, seeking someone to devour" (1 Pet. 5:8).

Lie 2: My trial and suffering mean God doesn't love me.
Truth: Nothing can separate me from God's love.
Scripture: "No, in all these things we are more than conquerors through him who loved us. For I am sure that neither death nor life, nor angels nor rulers, nor things present nor things to come, nor powers, nor height nor depth, nor anything else in all creation, will be able to separate us from the love of God in Christ Jesus our Lord" (Rom. 8:37–39).

Lie 3: My trial reflects my lack of faith.
Truth: My trial can prove my faith.
Scripture: ". . . though now for a little while, if necessary, you have been grieved by various trials, so that the tested genuineness of your faith—more precious than gold that perishes though it is tested by fire—may be found to result in praise and glory and honor at the revelation of Jesus Christ" (1 Pet. 1:6–7).

Lie 4: My trial produces only pain.
Truth: Trials can produce spiritual fruit.
Scripture: "We rejoice in our sufferings, knowing that suffering produces endurance, and endurance produces character, and character produces hope" (Rom. 5:3–4).

Lie 5: My trial is a waste of time.
Truth: My trial prepares an eternal weight of glory for me.

Scripture: "So we do not lose heart. Though our outer self is wasting away, our inner self is being renewed day by day. For this light momentary affliction is preparing for us an eternal weight of glory beyond all comparison, as we look not to the things that are seen but to the things that are unseen. For the things that are seen are transient, but the things that are unseen are eternal" (2 Cor. 4:16–18).

Lie 6: My trial is pointless.
Truth: My trial makes me more like Jesus.
Scripture: "And we know that for those who love God all things work together for good, for those who are called according to his purpose. For those whom he foreknew he also predestined to be conformed to the image of his Son, in order that he might be the firstborn among many brothers" (Rom. 8:28–29).

Lie 7: I'm alone in my trials.
Truth: My triune God is with me.
Scripture: (1) Jesus is my sympathetic high priest (Heb. 4:15–16). (2) The Holy Spirit is my Helper (John 14:26–27). (3) My heavenly Father loves me (1 John 3:1).

Lie 8: I'm the only one who suffers.
Truth: Christians suffer throughout the world.
Scripture: "Resist [the devil], firm in your faith, knowing that the same kinds of suffering are being experienced by your brotherhood throughout the world" (1 Pet. 5:9).

Lie 9: My trial will never end.
Truth: Whether in this life or the next, my trial will end.

Scripture: "And after you have suffered a little while, the God of all grace, who has called you to his eternal glory in Christ, will himself restore, confirm, strengthen, and establish you" (1 Pet. 5:10).

Lie 10: My trial is too strong for me.
Truth: God's grace is sufficient.
Scripture: "But he said to me, 'My grace is sufficient for you, for my power is made perfect in weakness'" (2 Cor. 12:9).

I stopped my list at ten, but so many more could be added. The fight for truth in trials is an ongoing one; however, it starts with identifying the lies we might not even have realized we were listening to and learning how to speak God's word—about his character, promises, and ways—back to them.

So far this guidebook to the off-road trails of motherhood has led us to acknowledge our hard realities, explore biblical lament, see how our stories are woven into another story, and navigate some of the questions that often travel with our trials. We've answered the question, "Is God still good?" Yes, he is still good, and we can trust him, his promises, and his ways. Knowing biblical truth then equips us to combat our enemy's lies. As we head into the final part of this book, we'll consider, in light of all these things, how God intends for us to live in our trials. It's time to look at the secret of biblical contentment.

Prayer

Dear Lord, thank you that darkness is not dark to you (Ps. 139:12), and you love to shine your light into the secret places of our hearts and minds. Thank you for exposing some of these lies that we have so easily swallowed, often without even realizing what we've done; now, help us fight for truth in our inward parts.

> Let the words of my mouth and the meditation of my
> heart
> be acceptable in your sight,
> O LORD, my rock and my redeemer. (Ps. 19:14)

In Jesus's name, amen.

Bible Verses

Job 1:22	Phil. 4:8
Pss. 42:5; 139:12	Heb. 2:18; 4:12
Matt. 6:25–33	1 Pet. 4:12
Eph. 6:17	1 John 1:9–10

Reflection Questions

1. If you weren't able to try the thought experiment, consider planning a time to go back and do it.

2. Of the ten listed lies and truths that are common to suffering moms, which one(s) do you struggle with the most?

3. Which friend helps you believe truth and would be willing to ask thoughtful questions when she sees you struggle? Consider sharing with her some of what you've learned about yourself and what's going on in your own head, especially as it relates to your current motherhood challenges.

4. If you could pick one of God's attributes to study further, to help you combat your own lies, which one would it be?

5. Consider photocopying the Lie and Truth Chart (appendix B) and putting it somewhere you can reference it frequently. (Mine is on the wall of my laundry room.)

9

The Secret of Biblical Contentment

I TOOK A PHYSICAL EDUCATION CLASS in college to fulfill a graduation requirement, and I still remember a multiple-choice problem that I got wrong on an exam. The question was: When running, where should a person look? I marked the letter next to the answer that said to look at the ground. It made sense to me. Shouldn't I look down to avoid tripping over tree roots, puddles, or whatever other obstacles might lie on my path? My teacher considered my case but wasn't swayed. While it's important to be aware of one's surroundings, the correct answer was that a runner should look straight ahead.

An athlete ought always to keep his or her eyes on the prize, and even if you and I move at a snail's pace on our journeys heavenward, so should we. Burrs might stick to our socks, brambles catch our shirtsleeves, and sharp curves require some fancy footwork on off-road trails, but our gaze should be fixed forward-facing.

However sharp our impediments feel when they poke us, we must resist the temptation to spend all our time staring at and trying to outmaneuver them. Instead, we ought to concentrate the majority of our energy on moving forward in this race, remembering who ran it before us travels with us, and waits for us at the finish line—Jesus.

How does God intend for us to live in our trials? With eyes on Jesus. That's why, in this final chapter, we're going to focus on following Jesus in our trials. And this is closely tied to biblical contentment.

A Secret Revealed

My daughter loves a secret, especially if it has anything to do with Christmas or an upcoming birthday. Her eyes sparkle, and a grin stretches across her face as she puts her finger to her lips and nods her head in a knowing way. She promises not to say a word to her older brothers about a package she spies on our front porch. Can you relate to her joy? How would you like to learn a secret about following Jesus in your trials? It's the secret of contentment.

The apostle Paul faced numerous hurdles of his own, and this is what he wrote to the Philippian church: "I have learned in whatever situation I am to be content. I know how to be brought low, and I know how to abound. In any and every circumstance, I have learned the secret of facing plenty and hunger, abundance and need" (Phil. 4:11–12). Moms who suffer know what it is to be brought low. We understand sorrow, wordless prayers, sleepless nights, and overflowing tears. We're familiar with need—whether it's physical, emotional, spiritual, financial, or some other kind. But do we know what it is to be content? Have we learned Paul's secret? It's right there in verse 13: "I can do all things through him who strengthens me."

Paul *learned* contentment. Not overnight, but over time. So don't feel pressure to figure out this secret by the time you finish reading this book. But here is more hope and comfort for you: no matter how much mom life does or doesn't look the way you imagined it would, you too can learn the secret of contentment. It might seem like a lofty goal, but it isn't an unattainable one. Through Christ, you and I can do *all things*—even suffer as moms and help our suffering children—through Christ who strengthens us. This is the secret to contentment in our motherhood trials, and it has everything to do with sticking close to Jesus.

Everything We Need

We have everything we need for the trials we face. How is this possible? Through Christ who strengthens us. God, who demonstrated his power in saving us, "has granted to us *all things* that pertain to life and godliness" (2 Pet. 1:3). Not only that, but he has given us "his precious and very great promises" to accompany us along the way (1:3–4). In Christ, we have everything we need.

We don't have to grieve as others who have no hope grieve, because we have the hope of Christ (1 Thess. 4:13). We don't have to fear, even if we walk through the valley of the shadow of death, because our good shepherd walks with us, and his rod and staff comfort us (Ps. 23:4). We don't have to worry when the storms beat against our homes. Why not? Because our lives are built on the rock (Matt. 7:25). We don't have to grieve, fear, or worry, but if and when we do, we look to Jesus. He is our refuge (Ps. 46:1). He is our shield (Ps. 84:9). He is the one who speaks calm into our storms. His power is our strength, especially in weakness, and his grace is more than enough and available whenever we need it (2 Cor. 12:9; Heb. 4:16).

With Christ, we have every reason—and all we need—to be truly content. But there's another huge reality. Our hearts are prone to wander, and wandering hearts so often lead to wandering eyes, and those roaming eyes frequently land on another woman and what she has or hasn't got. When that happens, there's one danger that poses particular risk to suffering moms, one that threatens our full experience of the sufficiency of Christ and the discovery and enjoyment of the contentment he offers. This is the danger of sinful comparison. Before we dive into further discussion of how to stay connected to Christ and the contentment he offers, it's worth considering how sinful comparison can lead us off course.

Glancing in the Wrong Direction

While comparison itself—a simple lining up of two things to observe similarities and differences—isn't sinful, it doesn't take much for it to become so. And it doesn't take long for sinful judgment, discouragement, complaining, and discontentment to follow sinful comparison. I learned this the hard way.

When our children were first diagnosed with Alpha-1, Scott and I shared one car, we had a newborn, and I was homeschooling. In a matter of weeks, I had to figure out how to coordinate appointments with four different pediatric specialists for multiple children, as well as manage regular bloodwork and administer daily medications. I spent hours on the phone—navigating the hospital system—to guarantee I scheduled appointments with the right doctors at the correct locations. I couldn't have imagined squeezing one more thing into our jammed schedule.

Then I'd see other moms with healthy children and think, "Wouldn't it be nice to drive my seven-year-old to sports practice instead of to the gastroenterologist? Wouldn't I prefer that my kids learn how to play an instrument rather than how to take inhaled medications? It would be lovely to wait outside of an art class instead of waiting for a nurse to lead my children into the doctor's office."

A voice in my head whispered, "Those other moms probably have their own parenting challenges too. You just can't see them." While that may have been true, I found myself wrongly wishing that *were* true, not so much for their sakes as for my own. I'm embarrassed to admit that as someone walking through sorrow, stress, and isolation, as someone who should have been the last to wish the same on anyone else, I wanted those other moms to feel the way I did. You see, I'd sinfully compared myself to them, my story to theirs, and both I and my story came up short. Somehow, I wanted to level the field. It wasn't so much that I wished to switch places as I wanted others to experience some of what I felt, and I wanted pieces of their lives.

You Follow Me

In the middle of my real struggle with sinful comparison, the Lord arrested my heart with a conversation that took place in the Bible between Jesus and Peter, and it reset my course. This was the third time Jesus's disciples recognized him following his resurrection, and John recorded how Jesus gave Peter three opportunities to reaffirm his love for his Savior—one for each of the times he had denied knowing the Lord. But it was what they talked about next that really caught my attention.

As Peter walked and talked with Jesus, assured of his Lord's full forgiveness and having restated his love and commitment to him, Peter noticed John. He asked Jesus, "Lord, what about this man?" (John 21:21). In Peter's question, I hear my own: "Lord, what about *her*? What about that other mom at the park? What about my neighbor down the street? What about the woman sitting across the aisle from me at church? What's her story, and how will it turn out? Will it be easier or harder than mine? Will she suffer more or less than I will?"

Jesus answered, "If it is my will that he remain until I come, what is that to you? You follow me!" (21:22). I wonder if his answer to anyone who asks such questions today is similar. This may sound harsh, but please bear with me in applying this idea to some of the tender places of the heart in order to make a point.

If it's the Lord's will that another woman's child be well and yours be sick, what of it?

If it's the Lord's will that another woman get pregnant easily and it takes longer for you, what of it?

If it's the Lord's will that her path be smoother than yours, what of it?

I cringe even writing and rereading those questions, but here's my point. Why does the Lord's will for another woman's life matter so much to us? It doesn't change the imperative: "Follow me!"

We may never understand why God says yes to one woman and no to us. God isn't bound to explain his reasons to us. But context matters. So does the speaker. When Jesus essentially told Peter not to trouble himself about John's story, he did so in the very same conversation that affirmed the love between them. And in light of our heavenly Father's love for us, demonstrated in sending Jesus to die on the cross and rescue us from our sin, we can trust him when he says that he doesn't withhold anything good from his faithful daughters (Ps. 84:11). If our good Father, who loves to give good gifts to his children (Luke 11:13; James 1:17), says yes to her and no to you or me, then he must have a greater good in mind. These are hard truths to swallow, but we can swallow them because we know the goodness of the one who first spoke them. It's possible to both lament our losses and delight in Christ's love for us.

By God's grace, our family's schedule has relaxed. Our children don't see as many specialists anymore, and the ones we do visit, we don't go to as frequently; this breathing space has allowed our children to participate in a variety of activities, some of which I didn't know back then would be possible today.

But another expression of the Lord's kindness was found in his gentle correction, showing me that sinful comparison only ever leads in a bad direction. Whenever you or I meander that wrong road, we find the way back in Jesus's injunction, "You follow me!" (John 21:22). Whatever else God chooses to give or withhold from us, only in Christ do we find strength to travel with contentment—no matter what comes at us.

Love God, Love Others

To sum up, don't look at the ground (at all of your obstacles), but also don't look around (getting caught in the comparison trap). Instead, keep your gaze fixed on Jesus. Let him write your story, and don't get consumed comparing yours to someone else's. Trust him to be enough when your friend has a husband and you don't.

Trust his provision even when your sister has a steady cash flow and you don't. Follow *Jesus.* This is the antidote to discontentment. It's also the source of true contentment. Because, as we already saw, we have everything we need in Jesus. Sinful comparison leads to discontentment, along with a host of other things, but following Jesus keeps our eyes where they need to be and allows us to walk even the hardest roads with confident hope.

Follow Jesus. *Abide* in him. *Hidden* in Christ. The Bible uses lots of phrases to express this idea of a life that is in step with Jesus and lived by his strength. But however you frame it, this is the obedient, abundant life that God intends for you to live right in the middle of your trials—even the ones that aren't going away anytime soon (John 10:10). How do we live this way? The same way we live the rest of the Christian life—by faith (see chap. 5), with hope (because of the gospel), and in love. "But the greatest of these is love" (1 Cor. 13:13).

Love drives it all. There's the synergistic love within the Trinity as God the Father, Jesus the Son, and the Holy Spirit love one another. Then there's God the Father, out of love for us, giving his beloved Son as our generous welcome into his love (John 3:16). And then Jesus invites us to abide in his love: "If you keep my commandments, you will abide in my love" (John 15:10). And what are the greatest commandments? Love God and love one another (Matt. 22:37–40).

We start by abiding in the love that Jesus has for us. That's why we repeatedly go back to the gospel, where God shows us the full extent of his love. That's why we surround ourselves with and immerse ourselves in those things that keep pointing us back to the gospel and God's great love for us—primarily his word, but also those things and people that keep us in his word. God's word, friends who speak it to us, and songs that lead us to celebrate it tether us to Jesus's love.

And like any other loving relationship, we spend time with the person we love. We talk, cry, and sing to Jesus. We delight in knowing he is with us wherever we go, all times of the day. His loving presence is always available for our enjoyment.

How we express and demonstrate love for God and others might look different based on the nature of our difficult circumstances, but the call remains the same. Love God. Love our husbands and children. Love our church families. Love our neighbors. Love the lost. If we're called to be full-time caregivers, much of our obedience will be hidden. Our love might look and smell messy. It might feel insignificant. But all of it matters, and God sees it all.

Our care for our children is vital work. In some seasons, it's the main work God gives us to do, and it's our primary mission and ministry. So let's serve them with the same fervent love that spurs us on when doing anything else for God's kingdom, and do it for him (Col. 3:17, 23–24)—in the strength he provides. Wherever you are, in whatever scenario you find yourself, follow Jesus—in love.

All the Way Home

Grief may slow us down, surprising us at unexpected moments. When it does, we lament, crying out to God for mercy. Our "Why, God?" questions might trip us up, but when they do, we ask the Lord to reveal more of himself. Our heavenly Father doesn't always answer our prayers the way we would like, but when that happens, we can be sure that he has a different, better purpose in mind—one that involves trusting him, one which keeps us humble and dependent on him to do what only he can do. On our difficult paths, lies tempt us to doubt and disobey, but we counter them with truth from God's word. Whether within or without, whatever slows us down, trips us up, distracts or torments us, we keep looking to Jesus and trusting that God is still good.

Jesus said that "the way is hard that leads to life" (Matt. 7:14), which offers unexpected encouragement to those of us who are familiar with hard roads. While being on a hard road isn't in itself an indicator that we're moving toward eternal life, when we traverse hard roads as believing women, we find comfort knowing that the heavenly way has never been easy. It's always been an upward climb. But the end more than makes up for every steep step and treacherous drop-off we encounter along the way. Weeping may last for a night, or a month, or years—but joy is on its way (Ps. 30:5).

If you trust the Lord as he writes your story, because of his greater story, you know yours will end well—because it will end with him. But the Bible promises more than a happy ending. It offers hope and comfort that's available for each day of your journey. As you and I surrender our stories, each minute of every day, and the children we fiercely love to the Lord, we "taste and see that the LORD is good! / Blessed is the man"—and each mom— "who takes refuge in him!" (Ps. 34:8). Yes, God is still good, and he is our true hope and comfort for the unexpected sorrows of motherhood, all the way home.

Prayer

Dear Lord, our hearts are prone to wander, and so are our eyes. Where we've compared our stories to others', please forgive us. Rescue us from discontentment and its bitter fruits, and help us to follow you wholeheartedly. Thank you that in Christ we have everything we need for our journey home to you. In the meantime, help us to live the lives you've given us with freedom and joy. In Jesus's name, amen.

Bible Verses

Pss. 23:4; 30:5; 34:8; 46:1; 84:9, 11

Matt. 7:14, 25; 22:37–40

Luke 11:13

John 3:16; 10:10; 15:10; 21:21–22

1 Cor. 13:13

2 Cor. 12:9

Phil. 4:11–13

Col. 3:17, 23–24

1 Thess. 4:13

Heb. 4:16

James 1:17

2 Pet. 1:3–4

Reflection Questions

1. What secret did Paul learn, and what difference does that secret make in your own life?

2. How does it comfort you to know that, in Christ, you have everything you need for your motherhood trials?

3. When have you found yourself caught in sinful comparison related to motherhood? What harm did it do?

4. How is God calling you to abide in his love in the middle of your difficulties?

5. What gospel hope and comfort do you take away with you after reading this book?

Epilogue

SOMETIMES THE MOST PRECARIOUS hiking trail unexpectedly twists and, suddenly, around the bend isn't another steep path but a breathtaking view. Sunlight, previously blocked by leaves and trees arching over our heads, now shines brightly over valleys, forests, and a distant lake or river below. We see for miles, taking in where we've been and catching a glimpse of where we're headed. In awe, we pause to take it all in, to study where our laborious steps have brought us. For a moment, we rest from our strenuous exercise, drink deeply from our canteens, and tell God how amazing his creation is and how wonderful *he* is.

As we finish this book, I invite you to do something similar. Whether you've been walking a difficult path for a while or you're only just starting out, I encourage you to slow down for a few minutes, to be still and remember that God is *God* (Ps. 46:10). He *will* be exalted in your life, one way or another. Before you do the next thing, can you see how the Lord has already led you, or when he even carried you at times? How has he spoken to your heart, through his word and his Spirit, in the more precarious parts of motherhood? Pause and thank him.

Jesus taught, "'Blessed are those who mourn, for they shall be comforted'" (Matt. 5:4). For us who mourn over sin, its effects, and how it plays out in so many various forms of suffering in our families, this is good news. For us who grieve over the brokenness in our homes and turn to Jesus, the comfort of his forgiveness and hope of restoration awaits. What difference do this gospel-based hope and strengthening comfort make as we feed, entertain, teach, and love the children he's given us—with their particular care needs, personalities, struggles, and concerns? All the difference in the world.

God doesn't give you or me grace to live another woman's life, and he doesn't give us grace for the lives we expected to live. But as we fix our eyes on Jesus and find our contentment in him, we can experience greater freedom and increased joy to live the lives we've actually been given and to mother the children God's placed in our homes. We can move forward with songs on our lips and prayers in our hearts as we look to Jesus.

That's what happened for my mom in an attic room more than forty years ago. The dark cloud that had descended over motherhood lifted. For the first time, she could truly enjoy being my mom and knowing me as her daughter without the heaviness surrounding my diagnosis squeezing the life out of her. And as I grew out of one back brace at a time, she saved nearly a dozen of them as a testimony to God's faithfulness, as reminders of his hand writing our story—not the way she would have liked, with full and complete healing, but one with great mercy nonetheless.

Those dire pronouncements that I would need surgery never came true, though there were frightening days when it looked like they would. Even though my front-to-back curvature started at almost fifty degrees, it never worsened; and in God's kindness, the side-to-side curves in my lower back and neck, though pronounced on an X-ray, have always balanced one another, giving an appearance of symmetry unless one studies my body shape very closely. But when I was younger, my parents didn't know how things would unfold. They didn't know that not only would I learn to roll, crawl, walk, and run, but I would grow up, get married, and deliver children of my own. What they did recognize was God's grace at work in our family, and that's what my mom wrote about in a birthday letter to me when I turned three years old in 1981:

> God continues to tie this family together under Him; I still believe His sovereignty and touch on your back have made all the difference in our decision to follow Jesus. . . . It doesn't get easier, but the love is greater.

In her motherhood trial, my mom experienced God working *all things* for good. Today, she traces back and testifies to a history of God's faithfulness. And I know that in my vertebrae, I carry a story of undeserved grace; what's more, God has rescued my soul and healed me of my sin. For both reasons, my parents rejoice and give God the glory.

I don't know how my children's stories will unfold, and I don't know about yours. Our families' stories may develop very differently. Certainly not all of them will end with a degree of healing in this present life, though we pray earnestly for it. But of this I'm sure: Jesus and his promises remain the same for each mom who follows him. Because of the gospel story told throughout

Scripture, we can trust him, and that means we can trust him with each word, page, and chapter of our stories.

As a mom, I find great comfort in the image of God as my shepherd, gently leading me as I care for my children. It's with this image that I'll close:

> [God] will tend his flock like a shepherd;
> he will gather the lambs in his arms;
> he will carry them in his bosom,
> and gently lead those that are with young. (Isa. 40:11)

The heart of our good shepherd toward moms like you and me is gentle. How much more so when we suffer and care for vulnerable children? He's patient, not rushing us. His words are kind not berating. His intentions are loving and nurturing. If he nudges us along, it's always for our good. And if he leads us off-road, it is better to follow him than walk any other path.

Pause to take in the view, and then keep following your Lord.

Appendix A

Go-To Bible Verses

WE'RE TOLD THAT "WHATEVER WAS WRITTEN in former days was written for our instruction, that through *endurance* and through the *encouragement* of the Scriptures we might have *hope*" (Rom. 15:4). In our motherhood trials, these words remind us that God's word extends true comfort—the kind that encourages us to endure for the long haul—and gospel-based hope. But when life is both hard and busy, how do we access this comfort and hope?

In the months after my children's diagnosis with a serious medical condition, there wasn't much time for extended Bible study, reading books, or even writing in my journal. With time, I tried to prioritize personal Bible reading and Sunday morning worship, but in the beginning, since one child was recovering from an extended illness, I wasn't even able to attend church. However, one thing I did served me well: I started a list of go-to Bible verses. Some of them the Lord brought to mind spontaneously; others I noted when reading God's word or (eventually) heard in a sermon. When friends shared verses with me, I added them to my list. Kept where I could locate them quickly, these truths were ready to encourage me—especially on my harder days.

Do you have your own go-to Bible verses? If so, do you need a few more for your arsenal, ready to strengthen you against the enemy's attack and offer you support in your moment of need? If you don't have your own, you're welcome to use mine to get you started. For the most part, the following Scriptures are presented in the order in which they came to me in that intense season of motherhood, but I've added a few subheadings.

Glancing at it now, it's interesting to note the emphasis on *trust* at the start of my list and *hope* near the end. Have key words or themes caught your attention as you've read this book or in your personal Bible reading? Are there aspects of God's character or particular promises that meet you where you live these days? Add relevant verses to your list so they're easy to find when you most need them. As you do, you can be sure that God's word will accomplish his good purposes in your life—even in your suffering (Isa. 55:11).

Trusting God

"Let not your hearts be troubled. Believe in God; believe also in me." (John 14:1)

"Blessed is the man who trusts in the Lord,
    whose trust is the Lord." (Jer. 17:7)

"Many are the sorrows of the wicked,
    but steadfast love surrounds the one who trusts in the
        Lord." (Ps. 32:10)

"Trust in the LORD forever,
for the LORD GOD is an everlasting rock." (Isa. 26:4)

"For thus said the Lord GOD, the Holy One of Israel,
'In returning and rest you shall be saved;
in quietness and in trust shall be your strength.'
But you were unwilling." (Isa. 30:15)

"And those who know your name put their trust in you,
for you, O LORD, have not forsaken those who seek you."
(Ps. 9:10)

"Trust in the LORD with all your heart,
and do not lean not on your own understanding.
In all your ways acknowledge him,
and he will make straight your paths." (Prov. 3:5–6)

"Trust in the LORD, and do good;
dwell in the land and befriend faithfulness.
Delight yourself in the LORD,
and he will give you the desires of your heart.
Commit your way to the LORD;
trust in him, and he will act." (Ps. 37:3–5)

"Blessed is the man who makes
the LORD his trust,
who does not turn to the proud,
to those who go astray after a lie!" (Ps. 40:4).

God's Presence and Help

"Fear not, for I am with you;
   be not dismayed, for I am your God.
I will strengthen you, I will help you,
   I will uphold you with my righteous right hand."
     (Isa. 41:10)

"Yet I will rejoice in the LORD;
   I will take joy in the God of my salvation.
GOD, the Lord, is my strength;
   he makes my feet like the deer's;
   he makes me tread on my high places." (Hab. 3:18–19)

"Nevertheless, I am continually with you;
   you hold my right hand.
You guide me with your counsel,
   and afterward you will receive me to glory.
Whom have I in heaven but you?
   And there is nothing on earth that I desire besides you.
My flesh and my heart may fail,
   But God is the strength of my heart and my portion
    forever." (Ps. 73:23–26)

"The LORD your God is in your midst,
   a mighty one who will save;
he will rejoice over you with gladness;
   he will quiet you by his love;
he will exult over you with loud singing." (Zeph. 3:17)

God's Sovereign Power

"'Ah, Lord God! It is you who have made the heavens and the earth by your great power and by your outstretched arm! Nothing is too hard for you. You show steadfast love to thousands, but you repay the guilt of fathers to their children after them, O great and mighty God, whose name is the Lord of hosts, great in counsel and mighty in deed, whose eyes are open to all the ways of the children of man, rewarding each one according to his ways and according to the fruit of his deeds." (Jer. 32:17–19)

"But now thus says the Lord,
    he who created you, O Jacob,
    he who formed you, O Israel:
'Fear not, for I have redeemed you;
    I have called you by name, you are mine.
When you pass through the waters, I will be with you;
    and through the rivers, they shall not overwhelm you;
when you walk through fire you shall not be burned,
    and the flame shall not consume you.
For I am the Lord your God,
    the Holy One of Israel, your Savior.'" (Isa. 43:1–3)

God's Compassion

"He heals the brokenhearted
    and binds up their wounds." (Ps. 147:3)

"He will wipe away every tear from their eyes, and death shall be no more, neither shall there be mourning, nor crying, nor pain anymore, for the former things have passed away." (Rev. 21:4)

Prayer

"Do not be anxious about anything, but in everything by prayer and supplication with thanksgiving let your requests be made known to God. And the peace of God, which surpasses all understanding, will guard your hearts and your minds in Christ Jesus." (Phil. 4:6–7)

"For we do not have a high priest who is unable to sympathize with our weaknesses, but one who in every respect has been tempted as we are, yet without sin. Let us then with confidence draw near to the throne of grace, that we may receive mercy and find grace to help in time of need." (Heb. 4:15–16)

Trials

"Count it all joy, my brothers, when you meet trials of various kinds, for you know that the testing of your faith produces steadfastness. And let steadfastness have its full effect, that you may be perfect and complete, lacking in nothing.

If any of you lacks wisdom, let him ask God, who gives generously to all without reproach, and it will be given him." (James 1:2–5)

"In this you rejoice, though now for a little while, if necessary, you have been grieved by various trials, so that the tested genuineness of your faith—more precious than gold that perishes though it is tested by fire—may be found to result in praise and glory and honor at the revelation of Jesus Christ. Though you have not seen him, you love him. Though you do not now see him, you believe in him and rejoice with joy that is inexpressible and filled with glory, obtaining the outcome of your faith, the salvation of your souls." (1 Pet. 1:6–9)

"So we do not lose heart. Though our outer self is wasting away, our inner self is being renewed day by day. For this light momentary affliction is preparing for us an eternal weight of glory beyond all comparison, as we look not to the things that are seen but to the things that are unseen. For the things that are seen are transient, but the things that are unseen are eternal." (2 Cor. 4:16–18)

Hope

"Therefore, since we have been justified by faith, we have peace with God through our Lord Jesus Christ. Through him we also have obtained access by faith into this grace in which we stand, and we rejoice in hope of the glory of God. Not only that, but we rejoice in our sufferings, knowing that suffering produces endurance, and endurance produces character, and character produces hope, and hope does not put us to shame, because God's love has been poured into our hearts through the Holy Spirit who has been given to us." (Rom. 5:1–5)

"For we know that the whole creation has been groaning together in the pains of childbirth until now. And not only the creation, but we ourselves, who have the firstfruits of the Spirit, groan inwardly as we wait eagerly for adoption as sons, the redemption of our bodies. For in this hope we were saved. Now hope that is seen is not hope. For who hopes for what he sees? But if we hope for what we do not see, we wait for it with patience." (Rom. 8:22–25)

"Let us hold the confession of our hope without wavering, for he who promised is faithful." (Heb. 10:23)

Appendix B

Lie and Truth Chart

Lie	Truth	God's Word
The trial is my enemy.	Satan is my enemy.	"Be sober-minded; be watchful. *Your adversary the devil* prowls around like a roaring lion, seeking someone to devour" (1 Pet. 5:8).
My trial and suffering mean God doesn't love me.	Nothing can separate me from God's love.	"No, in all these things we are more than conquerors through him who loved us. For I am sure that neither death nor life, nor angels nor rulers, nor things present nor things to come, nor powers, nor height nor depth, *nor anything else in all creation, will be able to separate us from the love of God* in Christ Jesus our Lord" (Rom. 8:37–39).

Lie	Truth	God's Word
My trial reflects my lack of faith.	My trial can prove my faith.	". . . though now for a little while, if necessary, you have been grieved by various trials, so that the *tested genuineness of your faith*—more precious than gold that perishes though it is tested by fire—may be found to result in praise and glory and honor at the revelation of Jesus Christ" (1 Pet. 1:6–7).
My trial produces only pain.	Trials can produce spiritual fruit.	1. Trials offer an opportunity to get to know God and his word better, trust his character more, and develop mine (Job 42:5; Ps. 119:71; Rom. 5:3–4). 2. Trials make me more grateful for Jesus who suffered on my behalf (Isa. 53:5). 3. Trials remind me that earth isn't my real home and increase my longing for heaven (Rev. 21:4). 4. Trials deepen my prayer life (Rom. 8:26–27).
My trial is a waste of time.	My trial prepares an eternal weight of glory for me.	"So we do not lose heart. Though our outer self is wasting away, our inner self is being renewed day by day. For this light momentary affliction is preparing for us an *eternal weight of glory* beyond all comparison, as we look not to the things that are seen but to the things that are unseen. For the things that are seen are transient, but the things that are unseen are eternal" (2 Cor. 4:16–18).

Lie	Truth	God's Word
My trial is pointless.	My trial makes me more like Jesus.	"And we know that for those who love God *all things work together for good*, for those who are called according to his purpose. For those whom he foreknew he also predestined *to be conformed to the image of his Son*, in order that he might be the firstborn among many brothers" (Rom. 8:28–29).
I'm alone in my trial.	My triune God is with me.	1. Jesus is my sympathetic high priest (Heb. 4:15–16). 2. The Holy Spirit is my Helper (John 14:26–27). 3. My heavenly Father loves me (1 John 3:1).
I'm the only one who suffers.	Christians suffer throughout the world.	"Resist [the devil], firm in your faith, knowing that the same kinds of suffering are being experienced by your *brotherhood* throughout the world" (1 Pet. 5:9).
My trial will never end.	Whether in this life or the next, my trial will end.	"And after you have suffered a little while, the God of all grace, who has called you to his eternal glory in Christ, *will himself restore, confirm, strengthen, and establish* you" (1 Pet. 5:10).
This trial is too strong for me.	God's grace is sufficient.	"But he said to me, '*My grace is sufficient for you*, for my power is made perfect in weakness'" (2 Cor. 12:9).

Acknowledgments

WRITING THIS BOOK TOOK community effort, and I'm grateful to each person who played a part in making it possible. First, Kim Boettcher, thank you for asking me to speak to the moms at church about the topic "Trusting God in Trials" a few years ago. That teaching was sown in tears, but it has reaped the fruit of this book (Ps. 126:5–6).

Thank you to my pastors and wonderful church family at Sovereign Grace Church in Marlton, NJ, for caring for me well through the sorrows of motherhood. You have helped bear my burdens (Gal. 6:2), and your comfort supported me.

Thank you, prayer team, for praying for each chapter of this book. The Lord used your faithful encouragement to strengthen me, and your labor was not in vain (Matt. 6:4).

Thank you to the dear friends who sent me on a writing retreat so I could immerse myself in this book and meet my deadline. Chapters 7 and 8 happened with your generous help.

Thank you, Megan Hill, for your friendship, prayers, and writing encouragement. You believed in this book and walked it through the submission process. Thanks to both you and Winfree Brisley for reading and sharpening the manuscript on behalf of The Gospel Coalition Women's Initiative.

Thank you, Todd Augustine, for your compassion toward the women of our churches and desire to provide resources that speak to their needs and sorrows. Thank you, Tara Davis—your careful edits refined this book. It has been a pleasure working with both of you and all the fine people at Crossway who moved this book through the publishing process.

Thank you, Mom and Dad. You gave me complete freedom to tell our shared story, and you read, cried, edited, and prayed over the manuscript with me. You turned my childhood bedroom into a writer's nook, and you cared for my children while I worked.

Thank you, children, for your patience, flexibility, and support on my writing days. Motherhood includes sorrow, but it's much more than that; being your mom is also one of my greatest sources of joy. And the joy far outweighs the pain. I love each of you so very much, and I absolutely *love* being your mom. I wouldn't trade this privilege for anything.

Thank you, Scott. Thank you for holding me and loving me through all the joys and sorrows of motherhood. This book is written for moms, but the truth is, as a husband and father, you've walked much of this hard road with me. Besides my Savior, I can't imagine a more faithful or devoted companion than you. And this book wouldn't have happened without your zealous support. I love you!

Thank you, Jesus. If you lead off-road, there's no better path. Thank you for walking behind and before and with me each step of the way. *Soli deo gloria.*

General Index

Scripture Index

Also Available from the Gospel Coalition

For more information, visit **crossway.org**.

TGC | THE GOSPEL COALITION

The Gospel Coalition (TGC) supports the church in making disciples of all nations, by providing gospel-centered resources that are trusted and timely, winsome and wise.

Guided by a Council of more than 40 pastors in the Reformed tradition, TGC seeks to advance gospel-centered ministry for the next generation by producing content (including articles, podcasts, videos, courses, and books) and convening leaders (including conferences, virtual events, training, and regional chapters).

In all of this we want to help Christians around the world better grasp the gospel of Jesus Christ and apply it to all of life in the 21st century. We want to offer biblical truth in an era of great confusion. We want to offer gospel-centered hope for the searching.

Through its women's initiatives, The Gospel Coalition aims to support the growth of women in faithfully studying and sharing the Scriptures; in actively loving and serving the church; and in spreading the gospel of Jesus Christ in all their callings.

Join us by visiting TGC.org so you can be equipped to love God with all your heart, soul, mind, and strength, and to love your neighbor as yourself.

TGC.org